A Londo

Secker & Warburg, London

A London Album

Roger Whitehouse

Early photographs
recording the
history of the city
and its people
from 1840 to 1915

Contents

For My Mother and Father.

First published in England 1980 by
Martin Secker & Warburg Limited
54 Poland Street, London WIV 3DF
© 1980 Roger Whitehouse
SBN: 436 57090 4
Design and production by Roger Whitehouse
Printed in Great Britain by W. S. Cowell, Ltd.

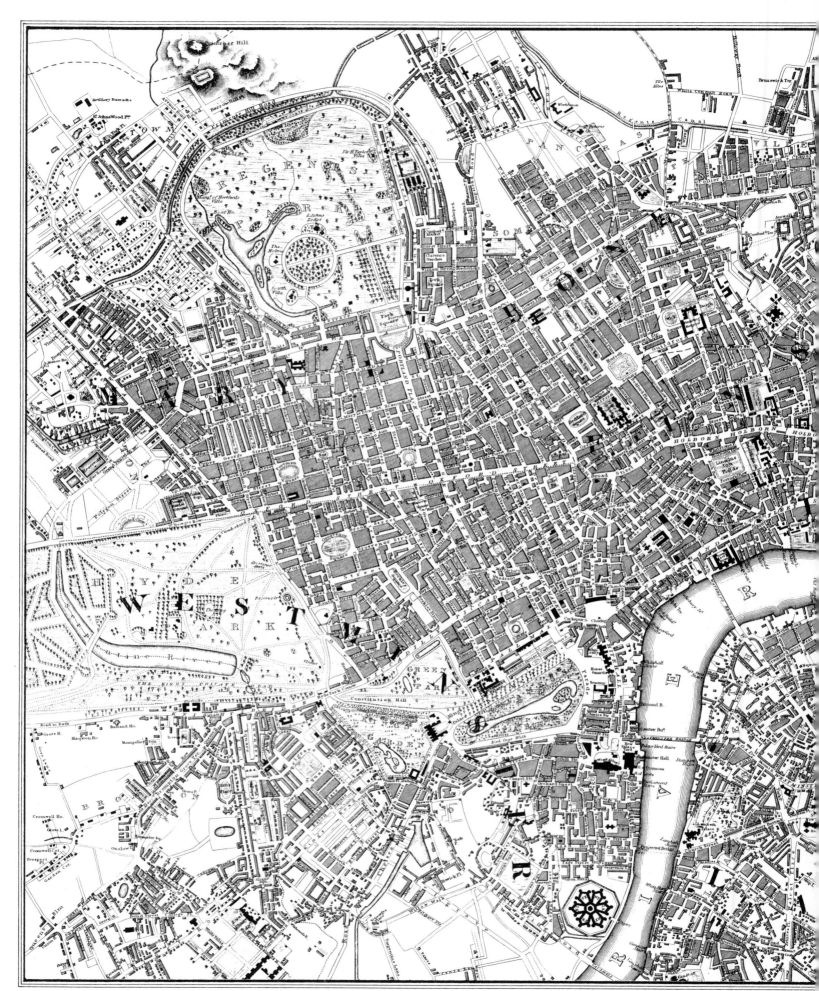

8. *United Kingdom Newspaper* map of London, 1832.

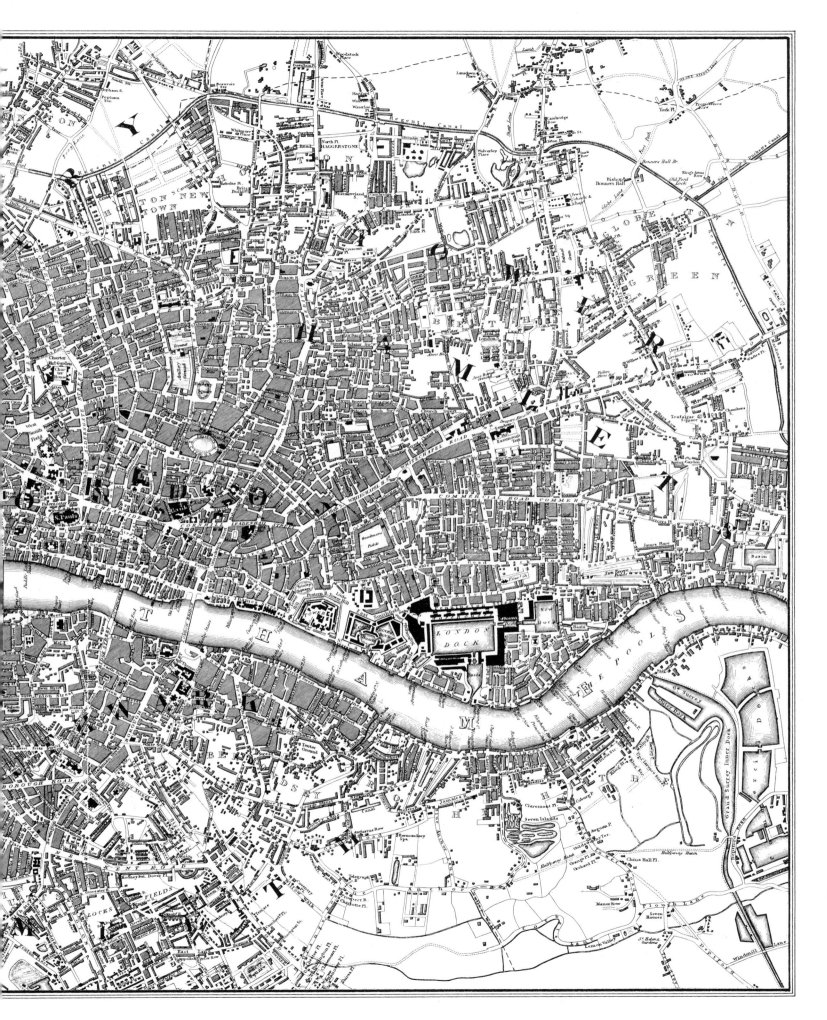

London: the first 2000 years

9. Bronze Helmet found in the Thames near Waterloo Bridge, c. 1st century B.C.

10. Bronze portrait of the Emperor Hadrian found in the Thames near London Bridge, A.D. 117-138.

11. Victory medal, minted in Gaul, showing Constantius being welcomed in London (LON).

Looking out over the towers and bustle of the modern city from the hills of Hampstead or Highgate we are well within the sprawl that map makers now label as London. Yet for most of London's history these hills were but landmarks lost in the haze well to the north of the city, often the destination for a day's excursion into the country. From the same vantage point about two thousand years ago, the view was of a wide, shallow, uncultivated and wooded valley which cradled the snaking curves of a great river as it wound its way to the sea below the distant horizon to the east. Occasional columns of smoke may have risen from some simple camps or dwellings, particularly from the areas upstream, evidence of some of the early inhabitants of the area.

Over thousands of years men have passed through or made their home here for various periods of time. Discarded stone implements from the dawn of history lie buried below the pottery and metalwork of the Bronze Age, whose warriors left a wealth of artefacts and weapons embedded in the river mud where they were lost in battle or cast as an offering to the gods. As new immigrant Celtic tribes arrived they brought with them new ideas and materials, including iron, in about 600 B.C. By the 1st century B.C. they were minting their own coinage, building fortifications and developing simple pastoral and mixed farming communities. There were probably no lasting settlements here yet, for without any permanent means of crossing the river there was not much geographical preference for one specific site over another. Yet this general area was of tremendous importance, for, after crossing the Channel at its narrowest point, anyone travelling inland attempted to ford the Thames at the first opportunity and it was here that the tidal effects of the sea became moderate enough (in those days), and the banks firm enough, to do so. These early Britons were far from being the woad-painted savages of legend but they were still a simple people with few belongings and, isolated from the mainland by an often stormy sea, were still very remote from the highly developed cultures that were well established around the more hospitable Mediterranean.

When the Romans, commanded by Julius Caesar, made their first temporary appearance in 55 and 54 B.C., they met considerable opposition in the area, particularly when they attempted to cross the river where the local tribes had built defences of pointed stakes. By the time of the next Roman invasion nearly a hundred years later in A.D. 43, the Thames was again vigorously defended but Emperor Claudius's army of well-trained men eventually succeeded in crossing. They established a low wooden bridge and formed a camp on the northern bank near the junction of a small tributary later known as the Walbrook. In doing so they had established the site of what was to become one of the world's greatest cities.

The conglomeration of buildings and activity around the bridgehead mushroomed to such an extent that by A.D. 60 *Londinium* was referred to by Tacitus as "filled with traders and a celebrated centre of commerce". In the following year, despite the ferocity with which Queen Boadicea attacked it, burned it to the ground and massacred its inhabitants, *Londinium* was rapidly reconstructed. The new settlement was built on a rough grid-iron plan superimposed over the network of Roman roads which spoked out over the countryside from the river crossing. At the end of the 2nd century, by which time it had become the capital of Britain, a great wall was built to enclose and protect its prosperous and cosmopolitan inhabitants. Seven well-defended gates gave access to its 330 acres crowned on the highest of two hills by the basilica where the senate met and court was held. Before the basilica lay a great open forum, over five hundred feet square, surrounded by colonnaded shops and administrative offices. Beyond, temples jostled with storehouses and the simple timber and thatch huts of the poor huddled around the elegant brick or stone homes of the rich. Besides re-creating a more familiar environment with red tile roofs, open courtyards, painted frescos, and rich furnishings, the wealthy Romans got some respite from the cold English climate with a system in which warm air circulated in ducts below the tessellated mosaic floors of their homes.

Despite their dramatic new concept of justice and administration and the complex network of cities and roads they had created, their empire was drawing to a close. Troops were increasingly recalled to defend positions closer to Rome and those that remained faced increasing opposition from bands of Picts and Scots sweeping down from beyond Hadrian's Wall. In A.D. 410 Emperor Honorius warned the cities of Britain that they would soon have to fend for themselves and shortly afterwards the last Roman troops marched away. In just three hundred years they had created the city of London, yet the walls they had built were to stand not only for the next six hundred years until the Norman conquest in 1066, but for six hundred years beyond that until much of them were pulled down with the debris of the Great Fire in 1666.

The next period of the city's history is shrouded in mystery. In the successive waves of invasion and migration from northern Europe, London was very often left unscathed when other cities were ruthlessly destroyed. In fact we are not sure whether London continued to function as a city or was deserted for a time. In any event its local and eventually international trading importance had recovered by the 7th and 8th centuries and after becoming the so-called capital of the East Saxons in 604, it was controlled by various Saxon kingdoms, occasionally being used as the meeting place for Royal Councils. Its proper revival may date from its deliberate re-settlement by Alfred in 886 after it had been left a smouldering wreck by the Vikings in 851. Alfred rebuilt the walls and may have been responsible for some street-planning during the reconstruction. In the 10th and 11th centuries the well-defended city and its army played an important part in the English-Danish wars and by the time of Canute, who opened up considerable trade by sea, it was well established as an important trading centre, a position it has retained ever since.

In this same period the city's two greatest churches were founded: St. Paul's, within the walls, established by the monk Mellitus, who was sent from Rome in 604, and St. Peter's, built in 785, as a simple timber structure on a remote area of the north bank of the river to the west of the city, consequently known as West-minster. In the belief that the site of the latter had been consecrated by St. Peter himself, Edward the Confessor set out to replace the primitive building with the finest church in all Europe. The great structure he built, some fragments of which still survive, was consecrated on Christmas Day 1065 and, as though to emphasise the importance of its construction as his life's work, Edward died a week later and was buried before the high altar. On the same day, 5 January 1066, Harold, last of the Saxon kings, began his short reign by being crowned there, initiating a custom which has been observed by all English monarchs since. Similarly, the little palace Edward had built to oversee construction of the church established Westminster as the seat of the English monarchy, an important fact in the future independence of London from the crown.

When Harold died at the battle of Hastings, William I (The Conqueror) had wisdom enough not to attack the city whose alliance would be essential for his success. Indeed the citizens soon conceded to the inevitability of his rule in exchange for a charter which simply confirmed their existing independence and he was crowned at Westminster on Christmas Day 1066, exactly a year after its consecration.

In those days Westminster was still an isolated area facing London across a giant loop of the river, the southern bank of which was open farmland with the exception of the cluster of buildings forming Southwark around the southern end of the much repaired and replaced wooden pile bridge. Within the great walls of the city itself, by now a patchwork quilt of repairs in many different materials, was a disorganised and often unsanitary jumble of primitive dwellings separated by a tangle of unpaved alleys,

12. A reconstruction of Roman London as it might have appeared in the early 4th century.

13. Old St. Paul's.

14. Panorama of London
from Bankside by
Wenceslaus Hollar, 1647.

15. Covent Garden,
engraving by Sutton
Nicholls, 1720.

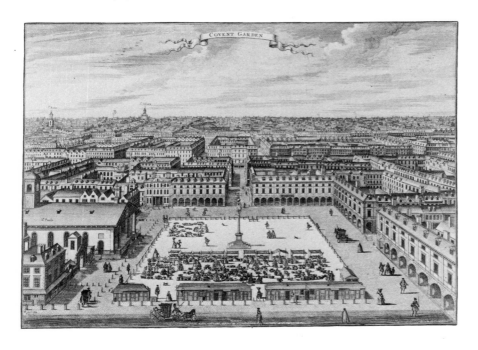

gardens, and irregular courtyards. Here and there the view was punctuated by the grander dwellings of wealthy merchants or wider streets where open air markets displayed an exotic selection of domestic and imported goods. The ships in which these goods arrived made the river-front a bustle of activity, from Billingsgate where fish and grain were unloaded, to Garlick Hithe where the scent of spices gave some respite from the otherwise often foul-smelling air.

But the Normans were great builders, and under their influence the irregularities of timber and plaster began to give way to the gleaming precision of new stone. Ostensibly to offer protection to the independent city, but no doubt more importantly to establish the power of the crown, William built three castles only the greatest of which, the Tower, still survives. By the time the Plantagenet dynasty began with Henry II in 1154, London abounded with new churches and monastaries including the cathedral of St. Paul's, although its great wooden spire, rising to the incredible height of approximately 460 feet, was not completed until 1222.

As always, the timber shambles that was known as London Bridge was threatening to fall apart from the increasing battering it received from the wheels of the wagons which fought with each other day and night to cross to the prospering city. As a consequence, in 1176, construction of a new stone bridge began. It was over nine hundred feet long consisting of nineteen irregular stone piers and pointed arches with a wooden drawbridge near the centre to allow larger vessels to pass. It took twenty-eight years to complete and though not unique, became one of the wonders of the world. It lasted over six hundred years until its demolition in 1832, less than ten years too soon to have given the first photographers an opportunity to record it.

Mediaeval London underwent considerable developments in civic government; its first mayor Henry Fitz Ailwin was elected in 1189. The 13th century saw both the signing of the Magna Carta after London's army had supported the barons against John's misrule and the beginning of the immensely powerful crafts, and later, merchant guilds. These guilds, founded to regulate prices, practices, and standards and to protect their members' employment from outsiders, have left a permanent mark on the city. Their meeting halls and

the streets named after their calling still survive as part of the modern city fabric. By then religion, too, had risen to an important and influential position as could be seen from the myriad of church towers and roofs which rose above the skyline. Further, apart from their religious function, the great monasteries, which now almost surrounded the city, were responsible for running the hospitals, schools, and other charities.

After the thirty-year Wars of the Roses were settled on Bosworth field in 1485 and the Tudor dynasty was begun, its second monarch, Henry VIII, brought about dramatic changes in the face of London. As a consequence of his quarrel with Rome, the dissolution of the monasteries immediately released London from the confining ring they had formed and a rapid expansion of the city into the surrounding fields began. Imposing palaces were built out along the unpaved track to Westminster known as the Strand (beach). The great Abbey there now became part of the Church of England and the palace of Westminster was established as the home of parliament. It is fortunate that Henry was such a great sportsman, for the areas that he reserved for his hunting, in order to protect them from the expanding city, became the great open spaces we now enjoy as Hampstead Heath and Hyde Park as well as many others. During this period London graduated from being just an important trading port on the fringe of Europe to being the centre of an international trade with a great merchant fleet. The ships that the city could muster were always an essential supplement to the navy, which Henry had created at Deptford early in the 16th century, and were usually very willingly given. When Spain threatened England in 1588 Queen Elizabeth received not the fifteen ships and five thousand men she had asked for but twice that number of vessels and six times as many willing hands.

By the middle of the 17th century London had become a very great and prosperous city, much admired throughout the world, and expanding rapidly in keeping with its success. It had long since burst past the confines of its walls which now lay almost totally hidden by the mass of new buildings which clustered around them. The ''East End'' was spreading rapidly beyond Aldgate, and on the other side of the city a thriving and elegant residential area already extended well past Lincolns Inn Fields to St.

Martin's Lane in the west and High Holborn to the north. At its centre, built on old monastic land and hence called Covent (convent) Garden, was a splendid new arcaded piazza, forerunner of a new type of residential development—the London square. To its south the city was built up as far as the great abbey at Westminster, adjacent to which the rambling conglomeration of buildings forming the Royal Palace had now been developed.

It was on a scaffolding outside the White Hall, after which the palace and the area were named, that Charles I was beheaded in 1649. Thus began the eleven year suspension of royal power during which Oliver Cromwell held sway until the restoration of the monarchy with Charles II in 1660. Behind the palace was the royal precinct of St. James's Park where Charles played *paille-maille* (a game not unlike croquet but on a course of crushed shells some 850 yards long) giving us the modern location and street names of Pall Mall and the Mall. It was here that Charles had given a house to Nell Gwyn and here that he was often seen, mixing quite informally with his subjects, walking in the park or even disrobing for a swim in the new canal he had built in imitation of Versailles. But the real focal point for those in search of some diversion, much of it bawdy, was over the river in Southwark. Clustering around the southern end of the bridge and reaching out along the river bank were an almost constant line of ale houses, inns, brothels, a bear garden and theatres including the Globe where Shakespeare had performed his plays from about 1586 until his return to Stratford-upon-Avon in 1610.

Other than by boat there was still only one permanent river crossing and that was the solitary and world famous London Bridge. Its nineteen bulky stone piers sat on even bulkier *starlings,* boat shaped constructions of wooden piles driven into the river bed and filled with rubble. These so restricted the flow of water that at low tide there was a difference of up to five feet between the levels on each side. The thundering rapids that cascaded between them made any boat journey downstream a sporting event and any upstream an impossibility. The roar of the water was added to by the churning and rumbling of the water wheels which pumped water up into storage tanks as part of the city's primitive water system. From here it was piped to conduit heads

16. The Globe theatre, Bankside, from Visscher's panorama, 1616.

throughout the city, about twenty in all, from which the several thousand members of the Honourable Company of Water Tankard Bearers delivered it fresh to the doorstep. In 1613 this was supplemented by a canal, called the New River, which brought water from Hertfordshire to a storage reservoir at Islington. Upstream, the partially dammed river formed a long placid lake in which the glittering panorama of palaces along the Strand and at Whitehall were reflected. From their steps stately gilded barges lazily put out to mingle with a multitude of rowing boats, eel ships and the many vessels bringing the city's wealth to the riverfront docks and warehouses. The relative calm of the water here often led to its freezing over and in severe winters it became the site of a frost fair where whole oxen were roasted over blazing fires set on the thick ice. Towering above it all was the bridge itself. Towards the Southwark end two great stone gateways controlled the only route to the city from the south. Both were usually surmounted by the heads of traitors, left to rot on long stakes as a salutary warning to those about to cross. The roadway, jammed solid with pedestrians and wagons, disappeared into the solid mass of shops and houses which cantilevered out over the water on each side and rose to such a height that only a central slit of light, five storeys above, illuminated some of the denser areas. In some places the buildings bridged the roadway entirely before opening out to give a sudden view of the river, by the gateways and wooden drawbridge and by the stone chapel of St. Thomas à Becket which until the Dissolution sat above the largest pier near the middle of the bridge.

For those who were fortunate enough to live on the bridge or in the houses bulging out over the water at the city's edge, sanitation was no problem, for everything fell or was thrown into the river below. But in the dense winding streets beyond, a choking stench pervaded even the remotest corner. On the many tiny and narrow sites timber framework houses rose ever higher, each successive storey cantilevering further out to gain every possible inch of floor space. In some instances the pointed gables which faced the streets were so close that the occupants could reach out and touch the building opposite. During the day the jagged slit of light high above could hardly illuminate the street below in the denser areas. At night, the only light, if any, came from lamps put out by individual householders wishing to dispel the shadows within which any form of danger might be concealed. As yet there was no form of regular police force and citizens had to protect themselves as best they could. Despite quite elaborate street cleansing regulations and the imposition of heavy fines, every kind of refuse was still thrown out of the windows above and the unpaved streets had become little more than open sewers cleaned only by rainstorms or the bands of scavenger dogs and pigs which roamed the city. Such conditions had encouraged so many to leave for the airier and sweeter smelling suburbs to the west that by the mid 17th century only one-sixth of the total population of about three hundred thousand remained within the walls. Wherever they lived, few could escape the ravages of the frequent outbreaks of disease unless they escaped to the countryside entirely. In the Plague of 1665 no one knows exactly how many died but it was probably in excess of a hundred thousand—more than one person in three. Over twelve thousand died in one week alone during the heat of September.

Despite all this, London was famous as one of the greatest and liveliest cities in the world. Although crowded, its buildings were much admired and among

17. Contemporary view of the Great Fire of London, 1666.

18. Wren's plan for rebuilding the City, 1666.

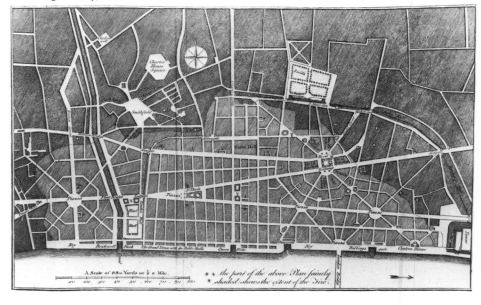

them rose over a hundred churches still dominated by the huge Gothic form of the old St. Paul's, now missing its steeple which had burned down after being struck by lightning in 1561. All around it, jammed between the buttresses, were the stalls and huts of the city's booksellers where most of Shakespeare's plays were first sold. In every street and alley, shops and carts created a gaudy display of expensive and colourful goods from all corners of the world. Here and there the first Hackney carriages were plying for hire but in these crowded conditions it was only the sedan chair that was nimble and manoeuvrable enough to make its way effectively through the endless jostling and cursing stream of horses, wagons, pedestrians and pushcarts. Even the nave of St. Paul's had become a public thoroughfare as the shortest route from Ludgate Hill to Watling Street and Cheapside beyond.

With the mass graves of the plague victims not yet a year old disaster struck at the city again. Early in the morning of Sunday, 2 September 1666, a fire started in a bakery in Pudding Lane, very close to the northern end of the bridge. Since fires were a fairly common occurrence in those days, not much notice was taken at first, but soon, aided by the tinder-dry conditions of the wooden buildings after an exceptionally parched summer, a brisk easterly wind fanned the flames into a raging holocaust. Before it was finally checked four days later (by blowing up the buildings in its path with explosives) the fire had left five-sixths of the city within the walls a heap of smouldering ruins and had progressed a fair distance west along the riverfront and Fleet Street. In one fell swoop the entire mediaeval city had been obliterated: the Cathedral of St. Paul's, eighty-eight churches, forty-four company halls, the Guildhall, the Royal Exchange, thirteen thousand, two hundred houses— all now lay strewn as rubble so thick that the average level of the area had been raised four feet.

While the hundred thousand citizens rendered homeless by the fire camped out in the surrounding fields and columns of smoke still rose from the ruins, plans were already afoot for the mammoth task of rebuilding. Thirty-four year old Christopher Wren was the first of many to submit his ideas to the king but his proposals and those of his successors, envisaging the replacement of the entire winding mediaeval street pattern with grand formal avenues, circuses and plazas, had to be rejected as impractical. Apart from the colossal expense that would have been involved in such a plan, there was no mechanism by which the land, often in thousands of tiny separate ownerships, could be surveyed, valued and re-apportioned satisfactorily. When reconstruction did eventually begin, the structure of the city reappeared very much as before although some opportunities were taken to open up the riverfront, make new connections and widen the streets. A law was passed which established that all new buildings were to be of brick or stone without oversailing upper storeys, laid down wall thicknesses and related the number of floors to the width and importance of the street. Wren, although not given the opportunity to fulfil his proposals for re-planning the new city nevertheless became one of the major forces in its creation. Not only did he build the new domed St. Paul's, but he achieved the near miracle of reconstructing more than fifty churches rebuilt after the fire.

At the same time that the modern city was taking shape the foundation of an even larger area of London was proceeding further west. The old country houses which had been built when land was still plentiful were now being assaulted by the rapidly expanding city and a new and novel type of development had appeared in response. In order to make capital of the very valuable land around them, and at the same time guarantee a suitable class of neighbour, the wealthy landowners began to develop rows of elegant uniform houses some of them forming squares around a common open space which often faced their family homes. The immediate success of these ventures saw them extending in the 18th century, west into Mayfair and Westminster and north above Oxford Street all the way from Edgware Road to Bloomsbury. The names of these squares, terraces, and streets remind us of the families whose considerable estates were incorporated into the city structure: Grosvenor, Cavendish, Cadogan, Portman, Portland and Bedford among many others.

Much of what happened in the century before the 1840s when Fox Talbot first recorded views of the city on paper negatives, survived long enough to be captured by the camera, and their story is therefore left to be told in the photographs which follow. As the map on pages VI-VII shows, the city had expanded considerably by 1832. Although Chelsea to the south-west and Hampstead and Highgate well to the north were still separated by open fields where cattle grazed and crops were grown, London, which by then was taken to include a great deal more than what was once enclosed by the city walls, had developed into a great and thriving metropolis. The old cities of London and Westminster, long since connected by an irregular tangle of 16th- and 17th-century streets, contrasted dramatically with the uniform terraces and squares of the great Georgian estates which comprised the western third of the city. The beginnings of Belgravia had reached out to entangle Chelsea, and Regent's Park and the street which Nash had built to connect it with the Prince Regent's palace in St. James's Park which had just been completed to the north. All these areas were of course the select enclaves of the well-to-do. The less fortunate, who in the 19th century arrived in the city by the thousands, accounted for the similarly dramatic growth of areas like Lambeth and Southwark south of the river and of course, their traditional home, the East End. The increasing hordes of vehicles and traffic of every description had made necessary the demolition of the city gates in 1760 and when, in 1832, the old London Bridge was finally demolished it was just one of eight structures which spanned the great river. The Thames had so long been solidly congested with the ever increasing mercantile fleets that a series of docks had been built down river, beyond the Tower, to enable them to unload cargoes from every corner of the globe. From there, the Regent's Canal, opened in 1820, circled the city in open fields to the north to connect the port with the great network of waterways throughout Britain.

But this was just the beginning, the first rumblings of a revolution that was to be far from merely industrial. The population of London, now the glittering centre of a great and expanding empire, had reached one million at the time of the first official census in 1801. By 1837, when the young Queen Victoria ascended to the throne, it had doubled, and by the turn of the century it would reach as many as five million. Such explosive change would demand new and radical measures in response and of necessity this was an age that would not hesitate to provide them. It is one of the fruits of the new age of science and discovery, the new born miracle of photography, that enables us to witness, first hand, some of the remarkable events and changes that were to overtake London and her inhabitants.

19-21. Three types of houses permitted under the Rebuilding Act of 1667.

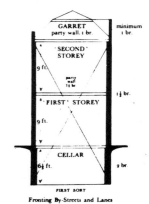

FIRST SORT
Fronting By-Streets and Lanes

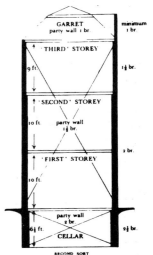

SECOND SORT
Fronting Streets and Lanes of Note and the River Thames

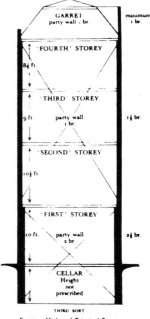

THIRD SORT
Fronting High and Principal Streets

XIII

Photography: a brief history

22. Camera obscura, c. 1646.

23. Early portable camera obscura by Jones of London, c. 1820.

The world of the early Victorians was still very much confined to an intimate knowledge of the immediate surroundings. The barriers of distance could be hurdled to some degree by a few hours journey on a stagecoach, steamer, or one of the new-fangled railways, or by turning to the pages of books and periodicals such as the *Illustrated London News* where accounts and sketches regularly kept an eager public informed of everything from the seven wonders of the world to events and personalities of the day. Imagine then the Victorians' sense of amazement at seeing a Daguerreotype for the first time in 1839 when it was made available as the world's first practicable photographic process. Here was not just a sketchy second-hand impression but one that retained in brilliant detail an image created by the actual light from the scene falling upon it. The fact that the process demanded, quite coincidentally, that the image be formed on what appeared to be the surface of a mirror, increased their astonishment even further; it was as if by some magic the normally fleeting reflection itself had suddenly and permanently become frozen on the silvered plate. No wonder that upon its introduction photography was immediately hailed as one of the new wonders of the world, not just another scientific toy but the fulfilment of a dream held since the beginning of history.

The development of a satisfactory photographic process had depended upon the solution of two separate problems: the optical one of causing the rays of light reflected by the subject to form an image, and the chemical one of creating a light sensitive surface to retain that image.

In principle, the solution to the first problem had existed since classical times in the form of the *camera obscura*, a darkened room with a pinhole aperture on one side which caused a rather dim inverted image of the view outside to be cast upon the opposite wall. Referred to by many scholars including Aristotle and Leonardo da Vinci, these were originally employed as a safe means of viewing eclipses of the sun. In the 16th century great interest was aroused in their application as an aid to drawing. This brought about the introduction of simple lenses to create brighter and sharper pictures and mirrors to enable them to be viewed the correct way round. Many of these *cameras obscura* appeared in the form of tents, sedan chairs, or even complete movable rooms before the artist was liberated from the dark recesses of the device's interior by the development of box-like portable versions and studio models in the 17th century. Although they continued to develop further during the 18th century, diminishing in size to be small enough to carry in the pocket or even be housed in the head of a walking stick, they had already progressed to the point where they could have been used for photography had a light sensitive surface been available.

The effects of sunlight in causing the fading of many materials and dyestuffs had undoubtedly been recognized since early times but it was not until the development of chemistry as a science that the more dramatic darkening effects of light on silver salts were observed. In Bavaria in 1727 Johann Heinrich Schulze discovered that a mixture containing nitric acid, chalk and silver discoloured quite rapidly in the light from a nearby window. To confirm this phenomenon he covered a bottle of the mixture with a stencil in which some letters had been cut, exposed it to light and removed the stencil to reveal the letters clearly imprinted on the liquid behind. Although the result was destroyed when the contents of the bottle were disturbed, this was the first recorded attempt of the formation of an image by a photo chemical process.

The two prerequisites for photography had now been established and at this point development continued along two separate paths. One, mainly in England, resulted in the negative-positive process still used today. The other, in France, although eventually to prove a dead end, was responsible for the world's first photograph and resulted in the creation of the highly successful Daguerreotype.

This cul-de-sac of development began in 1813 with Nicephore Niepce who, discouraged by his efforts as an artist, was experimenting with ways to directly produce lithographic plates by the action of light. He investigated substances which hardened rather than darkened on exposure to light and made many successful experiments in which he copied existing engravings by contact printing them onto plates coated with a thin film of bitumen of Judea. The soft areas, unaffected by light, were washed away with oil of lavender and turpentine after exposure. In 1827 after turning his attention to the *camera obscura* he exposed a bitumen coated pewter plate in one for an entire day to the sunlit view from his upstairs workroom window. The result was what is generally accepted as the world's first surviving photograph. More like a printing plate than a finished print, the image is not at all clear. Nevertheless, in the unretouched reproduction on the right, one can just make out the forms of rooftops and towers surrounding a central courtyard.

It was at about that same time that Niepce made the aquaintance of the theatrical designer Louis Jacques Mande Daguerre. In 1829 the two entered into a ten-year contract to develop the *Heliograph,* as Niepce called his process, although at this point Daguerre was only able to contribute an improved *camera obscura*. It was after Niepce's death that Daguerre discovered, in 1835, that the almost invisible image resulting from a relatively short exposure could be intensified by using mercury vapour to "develop" the silver-coated copper plates he was now using. With exposure time reduced from several hours to less than thirty minutes and with the achievement in 1837 of a satisfactory method of fixing the image with a common salt solution, Daguerre was ready to announce his new invention to the world. Thus, on 19 August 1839, details of the world's first practicable photographic process were revealed at a meeting of the Academies des Sciences and Beaux-Arts in Paris. The public was astounded. Most people received news of the miracle with unbridled enthusiasm; others regarded it with horror. A Leipzig newspaper, believing his invention an encroachment on the domain of the Almighty, denounced Daguerre as a fool and an agent of the devil. The artist Paul Delaroche could only remark "From today, painting is dead!"

The world clamoured for details of the new process and before the year was out over thirty editions of Daguerre's manual had been printed and sold out. Everywhere the first primitive cameras began to appear, usually consisting of two wooden boxes, one sliding within the other to focus the lens. This was still far from photography for the general public; only professionals and the most dedicated amateurs were left undaunted by the required inventory of over one hundred pounds of laboratory equipment and chemicals and the complicated process which followed. Briefly, a ready-made silvered copper plate was sensitized with iodine vapour to form a layer of light sensitive silver iodide. After exposure, the still invisible latent image was developed with mercury vapourised over a spirit lamp. The delicate positive picture so produced, formed by a whitish deposit of mercury-silver amalgam on the exposed areas, was then fixed in a salt solution, washed in distilled water and dried and mounted with an air tight seal below a cover glass to prevent abrasion or tarnishing.

The immediate popularity of Daguerreotypes resulted in much experimentation and within a year of its introduction additional sensitizing with bromine vapour and the development of much faster lenses reduced exposure times dramatically—from a quarter of an hour to less than a minute. With these improvements portraiture was now a reality although the sitter's head still had to be restrained with a metal clamp resulting in some of the typically composed expressions often associated with the early Victorians. Daguerreotype parlours opened everywhere to satisfy the enormous demand for quick and relatively cheap likenesses, many of which achieved a very high standard. Architectural and landscape shots became popular too, particularly in America, although exposure times rarely allowed moving figures or vehicles to register as more than ghosts. The process reached a peak of popularity in the early 1850s but despite its considerable delicacy and excellent detail, the demanding viewing conditions and inability to produce copies brought about its eventual demise by the end of the decade. The world's first practicable photographic process had proved a dead end; it was with another less popular system that the possibility for future development lay.

It came as something of a shock to the Englishman William Henry Fox Talbot when he received preliminary news of Daguerre's success early in January 1839 and he hurriedly made known his own experiments by submitting a paper to the Royal Society on the last day of that same month. Fox Talbot had begun several years before by making negative contact copies of lace and natural objects, such as leaves and feathers, on paper treated with silver nitrate and silver chloride. (Unknown to him at

24. The world's first photograph, taken by Niepce from a window in his home in 1827.

25. Daguerreotype in a case, c. 1850.

26. Daguerreotype camera, 1839.

27. Studio support, c. 1850.

28. One of Fox Talbot's mousetrap cameras, c. 1835.

29. A photogenic drawing made by Fox Talbot's method of 1839.

that time, Thomas Wedgwood of the famous English pottery family, with the assistance of Humphry Davy, the chemist, had made similar experiments at the close of the previous century but abandoned them for lack of a way of fixing the images.) In the summer of 1835 Fox Talbot had a number of very small cameras, nicknamed *mousetraps,* made up by a local carpenter and with them made many studies of his home at Lacock Abbey in Wiltshire. One of these, the oldest known surviving negative, is a tiny interior view of his library window and is still preserved in the Science Museum in London. In 1840 Fox Talbot discovered quite independently, like Daguerre, that the latent image produced by a relatively short exposure could be developed, in this case with gallo-nitrate of silver. His process consisted of coating writing paper successively with silver nitrate and potassium iodide to form silver iodide and then further sensitizing the material with the same gallo-nitrate of silver to be used again after exposure to develop the image. The paper was fixed with either potassium bromide or hyposulphite of soda resulting in a negative which was contact printed to produce a positive image. By 1841 the process had acquired the same short exposure times as the Daguerreotype and was patented as the *Calotype* although it was often known as the *Talbotype* in deference to its inventor. Despite the endless copies that could be made from one original, their tendency to fade, the strictures of the patent and the rather grainy quality of the prints made the process less popular than the Daguerreotype with its much desired ability to capture precise detail. However, since the materials were much lighter in weight, the Calotype process was well suited for travel, particularly in its later form with a waxed paper base which could be prepared some days before exposure and developed later. As a consequence architectural Calotypes were popular and one, by Fox Talbot himself, was taken early enough to record the finishing touches to the construction of Nelson's column in Trafalgar Square. Like the Daguerreotype the exposure time reduced street figures to a blur but in the controlled conditions of the studio, portraits were practicable and many fine examples survive, including those by the creator of the Calotype and by such masters as Hill and Adamson of Edinburgh.

Paper had only been convenient for photography because the sensitizing chemicals were easily applied to it; otherwise, its rough surface and fibrous structure destroyed detail, made printing laborious and gave a grainy effect particularly to the lighter tones. The use of glass as a base had long been considered desirable and had been prevented only by the lack of a satisfactory way to get the light sensitive materials to adhere to it. In 1851, Frederick Scott Archer, a sculptor and Calotype photographer, described a new process which was to supercede all others for the next quarter of a century. His *wet collodion* or *wet plate* process as it was known, employed a mixture of potassium iodide and collodion, a solution not unlike nail varnish, which was poured over a glass plate to form an even coating. When almost dried it was sensitized in a bath of silver nitrate and, still wet, was then exposed in the camera, developed immediately in pyrogallic acid, fixed, washed, and finally dried. The resultant glass negative was capable of excellent detail and from it an endless supply of prints of hitherto unattainable quality could be produced. This was true particularly when using a paper which had recently appeared on which the light sensitive materials were applied in a coating of albumen (egg white) giving a slight sheen to the surface. The wet collodion process had the added advantage of being able to produce direct positives in

30. The earliest surviving negative showing a window at Lacock Abbey taken by Fox Talbot in 1835.

31. Nelson's Column under construction in Trafalgar Square, photographed by Fox Talbot, c. 1844.

32. Calotype portrait of Sir William Allen by Hill and Adamson, c. 1847.

a variation known as the *Ambrotype* in which the negative was whitened with mercuric bichloride and mounted against a black background to produce something resembling an inferior Daguerreotype. A further and cheaper variation, known as a *Ferrotype* or *Tintype,* employed the same process but this time directly on the surface of a piece of dark enamelled tinplate.

The process may appear complicated but we must remember that the Victorians were great amateur scientists and loved dabbling with chemicals and equipment. In many ways, therefore, the more involved the procedure the more delighted they were, for the process itself interested them just as much as the finished result. In any event the dedication demanded of the early photographers was never better illustrated than at the time of wet collodion. They trudged over hill and dale not only encumbered with a heavy camera and tripod but also with an entire portable dark-tent containing bottles of chemicals, glass plates, tubes, dishes and an endless and weighty collection of bits and pieces. After locating a suitable stream for washing water and procuring some in a bucket, they set up both camera and dark-tent into which their upper half disappeared to prepare a plate. To complete their bliss, the atmosphere within consisted mainly of ether, the main solvent of collodion. One wonders how often on a hot Victorian summer day they were seen to slither gracefully to the ground wafted away on dreams of Fox Talbot or Daguerre.

Despite its technical complication the shorter exposure times of the wet collodion process made possible the beginnings of documentary photography. For the first time those at home were made aware of the actualities of war, not by means of the heroic gestures portrayed in etchings and paintings, but through the muddy and shattered landscapes of the photographs of Roger Fenton and James Robertson in the Crimea in 1855, or Matthew Brady and his team of nineteen photographers during the American Civil War in the 1860s. Although exposures were not yet short enough to stop action, the old rigid poses had relaxed into natural gestures held just long enough for the photograph, after which the subjects could go on about their business. This made possible semi-documentary photographs, such as those published in 1877 by J. Thomson in his *Street Life in London* (see plates 139, 172, 180).

In the high street studios the process was bringing about another revolution. In 1854, a Parisian photographer had patented a method whereby eight small photographs were taken in a special camera on one plate; this was then contact-printed onto one sheet of paper and cut up into eight small prints, four inches by two and a half, each of which was mounted individually on a card. Known because of their size as *cartes-de-visite* (visiting cards), they rapidly became a gigantic craze. Elaborate, often very ornate, albums were sold to hold them and the larger four by five and a half inch *cabinet* prints which appeared in the late 1860s. It soon became necessary to go around the entire family making sure everyone from Grandpa to little Ruby was duly photographed and their pictures distributed. Enterprising photographers obtained permission to take portraits of famous personalities for sale to the public and this rapidly developed into a very lucrative business. It is said that one *carte* of the Princess of Wales alone sold over three hundred thousand copies. This phenomenon underlined the vast social changes that were taking place. Although inconceivable twenty-five years before, the average working family could now afford not only a portrait of

33. An ambrotype of the author's great, great grandfather with the backing half removed to show how the positive image is created, c. 1855.

34. A portable wet-plate dark tent, c. 1860.

35. "In the Redan", an albumen print taken by James Robertson during the Crimean War, c. 1855.

themselves but an identical picture of the Queen herself which could be included alongside their own as a member in the family album.

In the same way that *cartes* introduced the Victorians to the famous, another craze brought scenes of distant cities and landscapes into their homes. Queen Victoria had seen some stereoscopic photographs at the Crystal Palace in 1851 and within three months a quarter of a million viewers had been sold in England and France. The process consisted of two photographs taken a few inches apart, recreating the differing view seen by each eye. When prints of these were mounted on a card, and placed in a special viewer which focused each eye on the corresponding print, the brain reassembled the slightly different images very realistically into a single three-dimensional picture. While examples of stereo Daguerreotypes do exist, it is with the wet collodion process that the system came into its own. The London Stereoscopic Company advertised a stock of over one hundred thousand different views for sale in 1858. Due to the small size of the prints, about three inches square, lenses could be employed of sufficient speed to reduce exposures to a quarter of a second and make possible the first real action shots, despite the frequent blurring of fast moving objects. They arrived just soon enough in the 1850s to preserve for us street scenes of a world now totally lost, of top hats and crinolines, hansom cabs and cobbled streets (see plates 50, 78, 83). Other popular examples include studio poses which show how the other (upper) half lived and comic or ''naughty'' views of what went on in the ladies' boudoir. However contrived, they provide a unique insight into life at the time and several are included in this book. Though not necessarily taken in London, the photographs clearly refer to life in the metropolis (see 117-121).

Frequent attempts were being made to liberate the photographer from having to prepare and develop the plates at the same time as the exposure. If the collodion was allowed to dry, it became extremely slow and in an attempt to keep the coating on the plate wet, ingredients, such as sugar, tea, beer, sherry, treacle, honey and ginger wine were introduced, adding the dangers of intoxication and obesity to the already anaesthetic effects of the darkroom. Dr. Richard Leach Maddox, whose health was becoming seriously jeopardised by the effects of ether, was the first to experiment with a dry gelatin-silver bromide ''emulsion'' but although plates of this type were marketed in 1873 they were still much too slow for any commercial success. In 1874 it was accidentally discovered that heating the same emulsion in order to assist the drying process, increased its speed considerably. By applying heat for a longer period the sensitivity of the plates not only matched the now doomed wet collodion process but reduced exposure time from half a second to an unheard of one twenty-fifth of a second. By 1879-80 the new dry plates were generally accepted and photography had made a dramatic advance. Up until that time cameras had changed little, consisting solely of a lens, a device for controlling the aperture, a focusing mechanism (such as bellows) and a ground-glass screen. The photographer had made the exposure, stopwatch in hand, by simply uncapping the lens. Now, with the introduction of exposures of fractions of a second, the tripod and ground-glass screen could be dispensed with and a shutter and viewfinder added. Views not only began to fill with figures and activity but these soon became a subject in themselves. Posing was no longer necessary and, in fact, it became the photographer's aim to avoid

36. Carte-de-visite of Queen Victoria and the Prince Consort, 1861.

37. Back of a typical carte-de-visite.

38. Stereo-card of Cheapside, c. 1896.

39. Stereoscope on stand, c. 1885.

any suggestion of it by catching the subject unaware. As the idea of "candid photography" spread, equipment was designed to be as unobtrusive as possible and cameras appeared disguised as packages or even more covertly concealed in the clothing with the lens projecting through a button hole.

Although dry plates had extended its range considerably, the equipment and skill required, while much simplified, still restricted the use of photography to professionals and dedicated amateurs. Clearly, what was needed now was a lightweight transparent base for the photographic emulsion so that the camera could become much lighter and easier to manipulate. In America in 1881 George Eastman had founded a company to produce dry plates and was busy trying to find a solution to the problem. In 1883 he introduced a paper negative roll with some success and two years later produced *American Film,* a paper base with a thin film of collodion and emulsion which was stripped off after development and mounted on glass to form a rigid negative. Still not satisfied he employed a chemist, Henry N. Reichenbach, to create a flexible transparent base for his photographic emulsion. After three years of experimentation and development with cellulose nitrate, Eastman Transparent film was finally made available in 1889, introducing a material which has remained virtually unchanged until the present day. But this had not been Eastman's only interest. At the same time he developed and introduced, in June 1888, a black box measuring just 3¾" by 3¾" by 6½" calling it, simply, the *Kodak.* Compared with everything that had gone before, this camera's operation was reduced to the level of absurd simplicity. It arrived already loaded with a roll of film sufficient for one hundred two and a half inch diameter circular exposures. The shutter was set by pulling a string emerging from a hole in the top; one aimed it, pressed the button and when the film was used up the entire camera was returned to Eastman, where it was opened, reloaded, and returned complete with the developed film and prints. The slogan with which Eastman promoted the camera, "You press the button, we do the rest", meant that now anyone could, and did, take "snapshots". Although often characterised by blurred and decapitated family groups they have probably provided for us a more accurate picture of the commonplace than any a more expert and prejudiced eye could have produced. Many of the photographs that follow were taken by amateurs (see plates 176, 177, 228) while others are by such photographers as Paul Martin (see plates 129, 137, 160) who, by exploiting the flexibility of the new medium, took many candid views of Londoners in the 1890s and pioneered the technique we now know as photo journalism.

The only remaining obstacle to the mass acceptance of photography was cost, and this was removed with the introduction of the first *Brownie* in 1900 which sold for just one dollar. With the arrival of the 20th century, photography had in just sixty years been transformed from a complex miracle into an everyday event.

No matter how commonplace photography may have become today, few can deny the magic of seeing in these old prints the events and inhabitants of a past age viewed across the gulf of the intervening years. Perhaps in our mind's eye we can follow these men, women and children about their business among the noise and bustle of a strange sounding and strange smelling London after that one frozen moment that has been snatched out of time by the camera shutter.

40. Lancaster Instanto-graph Camera, with a rubber-band operated shutter, 1896.

41. Kodak Number One Camera, 1888.

42. Circular print from a Kodak Number One Camera, c. 1890.

43. Girl with a Kodak "Brownie", c. 1901.

When the pioneer photographers first exposed glass and paper plates to views of London in the early years of Victoria's reign, it was still so small that a few miles' walk in any direction brought one to isolated villages and open fields: open that is, but for the scaffolding and piles of building materials being used for its already accelerating expansion. On the outskirts, well ordered squares and terraces formed a dignified setting for the equally well ordered lives of well staffed and well run households. In the older areas of the city, an informal jumble of three-, four- and five-storey buildings of wood, brick and stone crowded along winding streets that bustled with activity. Everywhere the cries of the street traders and cabbies were barely audible above the constant and incredible din of steel-shod hoofs and steel-rimmed wheels thundering against stone pavings. The prints in this first chapter are selected mainly from this early period. They show a London still very much rooted in the past; buildings of a much more domestic scale form the background to an age of top-hats and crinolines about to be swept away forever by the oncoming tide of social and technological change.

44. St. Paul's Cathedral, looking north-west from Southwark Bridge, c. 1859. Seen here when it still towered above the old buildings of the City, Sir Christopher Wren's masterpiece was the third cathedral to be built on this site and was completed in 1710, replacing the old cruciform structure (see page IX) destroyed during the Great Fire. In the foreground, to the left, a group of men relax on the river steps in front of Queenhithe. This little inlet, which in earlier times had equalled Billingsgate in importance as a landing place (particularly for corn), eventually fell into decline due to its location above the considerable obstacle to shipping created by the old London Bridge. This view illustrates well the maze of wharfs, alleys, warehouses, factories and inns along the waterfront which formed the background to a colourful and long lost way of life centered on the river.

Old London

"One day Father took us into Town to see the ice on the Thames. We stood on Hungerford Bridge and saw the floes drifting down and piling up above Waterloo Bridge and were told that some men had crossed from the south side to the Embankment on the ice."

From "Drawn from Memory" by Ernest H. Shepard.

45

46

London would never have existed were it not for the river. Its original site came about as the most convenient crossing place and its growth and prosperity was determined by its suitability as a major port. In the 19th century the Thames still provided the easiest means of transport between east and west and was consequently a scene of constant activity.

45. On board a Thames sailing barge, 1884.

46. "Workers on the Silent Highway", c. 1877.

47. The Houses of Parliament, looking north-west across the frozen river from Lambeth, winter 1892.
Ice on the Thames was a common sight before the 20th century, due both to the colder temperatures then and the dam-like effect of the old London Bridge which stood until 1832. In those days frost fairs were often held on the ice complete with oxen-roasting and every kind of entertainment. Note the heavily laden hay-barge on the left bringing food for some of the tens of thousands of horses that were still the principal form of power and transport on land.

48. Shipping on the Thames, c. 1880.
Large ocean-going vessels, sailing-barges and twin-funnelled steam-tugs competed for space on the busy river near Gravesend.

49. Wapping quayside, c. 1860.
At low tide the masts and rigging assumed even more chaotic positions as these old wooden hulls settled down onto the Thames mud.

50. Greenwich Pier, looking west, 1857.
The first steamboat had appeared on the Thames in 1815. By the 1850s the river was alive with these tall-funnelled paddle-steamers, and by 1870 it was estimated that twenty million passengers travelled this way each year. From here, as from many other landing places along the river, a continuous quarter-hour timetable carried thousands of passengers to and fro on pleasure and business. Beyond the diamond-patterned funnel on the right (each line had its own special markings) is one of the several old hulks of men-of-war, now bereft of their rigging, which were used as prison ships, police stations and quarantine quarters (see plates 207-208).

48

49

50

The docks

With the enormous volume of traffic created by a prosperous economy, the twenty legal quays between London Bridge and the Tower and the "sufferance" wharfs opposite became seriously overcrowded, forcing rows of vessels to queue up in midstream waiting to unload their cargoes. Although private wet docks had existed as early as the 17th century it was not until 1799 that an Act of Parliament broke the City's monopoly allowing new docks to be built downstream. The giant West India Docks were rapidly cut across the Isle of Dogs and opened in 1802, followed by the London Docks at Wapping in 1805. By the end of the century many others had been added, creating the largest system of docks in the world.

51. Unloading a merchantman, London Docks, 1895.

52. The South West India Docks, c. 1885.

53-54. The vaults at the London Docks, 1895.
Constant arrivals of wine and brandy were sampled and gauged to determine the exact contents and volume of the barrels before they were stored in the acres of bonded vaults below. The black spongy fungus hanging from the ceiling is a growth peculiar to wine cellars.

52

"In the far distance, behind the interminable lines of sheds and warehouses, masts bound the horizon, masts like a bare forest in winter, finely branched, exaggerated, aerial trees grown in all the climates of the globe."

From "Highways and Byways in London", 1902.

51   **53**

54

Landmarks

55. St. Paul's Cathedral from the air, May 1909.

56. Temple Bar in the Strand, looking west, 1878. Seen here in the year of its removal, Temple Bar, built in 1672, marked the boundary of the City and Westminster. Through the arch are Wych Street (see next page), St. Clement Danes Church and the hoardings marking the site of the new Law Courts.

57. Cannon Alley, looking south toward St. Paul's from Paternoster Row, c. 1900. When architectural scale was consistent with function, the term landmark was often a literal one, for the churches and monuments which dominated the skyline could be used as reference points among the winding streets and alleys. Note the inclined mirrors which were hung outside the windows in an attempt to reflect some light into gloomy lower rooms.

58. The Monument, looking east along Arthur Street (now Monument St.), across Fish Hill Street, c. 1880. Commemorating the Great Fire of 1666, the 202-foot column dwarfs the buildings which formed a square around its base before their demolition in 1887 to extend Monument Street.

56

57

58

Tudor relics

59. 16th-century houses in Bermondsey Street, 1893.

60. Early 17th-century houses in Wych Street, looking east toward the Strand, 1876. Wych Street, demolished in 1899 to make way for the Aldwych, had one of the finest collections of overhanging Tudor houses in London. Over the rooftops is the tower of St. Clement Danes (see previous page).

61. The Sir Paul Pindar Tavern, Bishopsgate, 1877. Sir Paul Pindar, diplomat and merchant, began building the house, of which this wooden front was only a part, in 1599 during the reign of James I. It became a tavern in the 18th century and is seen here in the year it was demolished to make room for the enlargement of Liverpool Street Station. The façade still survives in the Victoria & Albert Museum.

62. Staple Inn, on the south side of Holborn, 1865. Built in 1586 this was one of the nine Inns of Chancery through which students traditionally passed before entering one of the four Inns of Court. It is seen here covered in stucco before the renovation of its half-timbering in 1866. It still survives, restored again after its devastation by a flying bomb in 1944.

60

61

62

64

65

63. The south entrance to St. Helen's Church in Great St. Helen's, off Bishopsgate, 1886. Known as the "Westminster Abbey of the City" this church has a history dating back to Saxon times. It became part of a Benedictine nunnery in the 13th century from which period much of the structure dates.

64. Cloth Fair, West Smithfield, 1877.
These old Elizabethan and Jacobean houses, clustered around the church of St. Bartholomew-the-Great, were inhabited by old clothes dealers and rag and bone merchants until they were demolished in 1900 as a health hazard.

65. Storage vaults beneath the Adelphi, c. 1900.
Situated just south of the Strand, the Adelphi was built by the Adam brothers between 1768 and 1774 as a bold piece of residential speculation. Below the elegant terrace were 265-foot-deep storage vaults leading directly from the quayside and intended originally for lease as an arsenal. However, due to general dampness and frequent flooding, they were unsuitable for such a purpose and in reality became a refuge for the destitute.

Coaching inns

Before the age of steam, long-distance journeys took many days, requiring regular stabling for both passenger and horse. The resultant building form, mediaeval in origin, universally consisted of courtyards behind a conventional façade surrounded by galleries leading directly to the guests' rooms.

66. The George Inn, Southwark, 1889.
Many visitors stopped here, or in one of the other twenty-two inns in the vicinity of Borough High Street, in the days when London Bridge was so crowded that it was extremely difficult for large coaches to proceed any further. First mentioned as early as 1554, the George was rebuilt after the Southwark fire of 1676 when it perished along with six hundred other structures. It is now the only remaining example of its type.

67. The courtyard of an inn in Bishopsgate, 1865.
Although originally open, the galleries of many inns were screened in to provide more shelter.

68-69. The upper gallery and stables of the Oxford Arms in Warwick Lane, 1875. Situated hard by St. Paul's, this inn, rebuilt after the Great Fire, was a landmark for many years until its demolition in 1876.

67

69

68

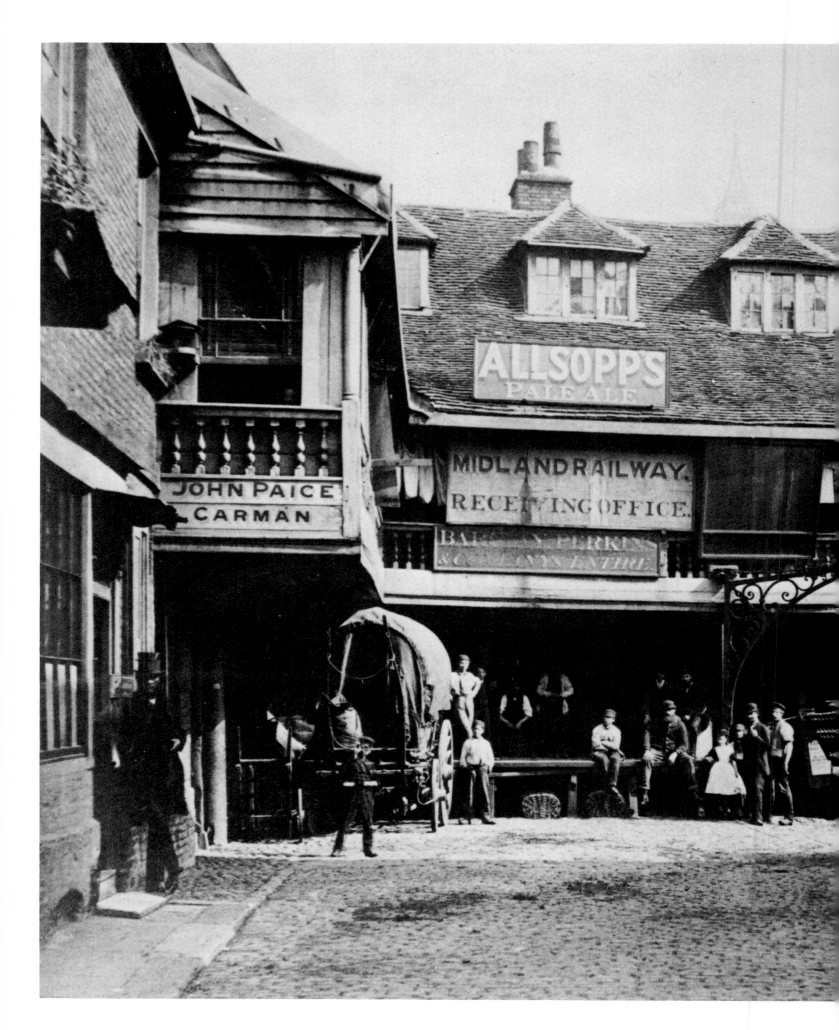

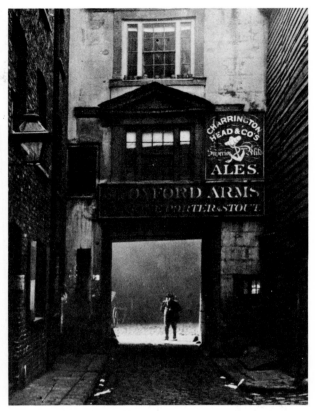

70. The Talbot (originally the Tabard) Inn, Borough High Street, Southwark, c. 1865. Probably the most famous inn of London, the Tabard was immortalised by Chaucer as the starting point of his twenty-nine pilgrims. It was destroyed, along with the original George nearby, in the Southwark fire of 1676 and was reconstructed afterwards as the Talbot. As coaching declined the extensive stables of many inns became depots for the railway and carrier companies, and the rooms were frequently let out as tenements.

71. The entrance to the Oxford Arms, Warwick Lane, 1875. It was the imminent destruction of this building (see plates 68-69) which prompted the formation of the Society for Photographing Relics of Old London. This, and many other photographs in this book (see plates 60, 63, 64, 99), are a result of their endeavours.

The City

The City of London today marks the location of the original Roman, and most of the mediaeval, capital. Although the entire population once lived here, as it grew more crowded those who could afford to left to take up residence in the adjacent Royal City of Westminster leaving commerce to take their place.

72. Looking east along the Strand toward the City from the Law Courts, c. 1894. The monument by Sir Horace Jones, in the centre of the Strand, marks the boundary of the City and site of the old Temple Bar (see plate 56). The Law Courts on the left, designed by G.E. Street, were built between 1874-82.

73. Looking east from the roof of the Mansion House along Threadneedle Street, 1901. The Bank of England (left) by Sir John Soane was completed in 1833. The interior was demolished in 1924 and replaced to the designs of Sir Horace Baker. The Royal Exchange (centre) was designed by Sir William Tite on the site of an earlier cloistered structure.

74. Looking east along Fleet Street toward Ludgate Circus and St. Paul's Cathedral, c. 1897.

75. Davidson Newman & Co., Leadenhall, c.1900.

73

74

75

76. Ludgate Hill, looking east, c. 1902.
This view affords us a rare glimpse into the well padded interior of a hansom cab (see plate 222) as the passenger doors, which the driver controlled with a lever, are open waiting for a fare. The only shelter against the elements for the cabbie was provided by an oilcloth which can be seen rolled up on top of the cab. Similar protection was provided for the driver and front passengers on the top of the bus waiting alongside.

77. Bennett's clock shop, 64-5 Cheapside, 1891.
A City landmark for many years, this specially built shop front contained eight different clock faces displaying the time in different parts of the world. It also housed two bell alcoves, the figures in the lower one representing Gog and Magog, and was topped by a giant six-foot-diameter ball on the roof which was dropped down its supporting pole each midday exactly on the hour. When it was demolished in 1929, the figures were bought by Henry Ford and installed in the Edison Institute at Greenfield, Michigan.

79

78

Whereas the City was still confined to the old street patterns rebuilt after the fire, the newer extensions of London to the west were much better appointed with wider streets and many public open spaces.

78. Haymarket, looking north from Pall Mall, c. 1861.
The portico on the right, just beyond Suffolk Place, is that of the Haymarket Theatre. Facing it across the street is the original Her Majesty's Theatre eventually destroyed by fire in 1867 (see plate 214).

79. Trafalgar Square, looking south-west, c. 1870.
Originally suggested by Nash, a square was formed here on the site of the Royal Mews in 1830. The Nelson column by William Railton was added in 1840 and the Landseer lions in 1867.

80. Trafalgar Square, looking north-west, c. 1900.
Taken at the turn of the century as a demonstration shot on a novel new Kodak panoramic camera.

81. Piccadilly Circus, looking west, c. 1900.
Canvas awnings shade the shop fronts along Piccadilly, named after Piccadilly House, the home of a manufacturer of shirt frills or ''Pickadills'' which was originally situated here.

80

81

Regent Street

In 1811 John Nash submitted his original proposals for a "Royal Mile" to connect the Prince Regent's official residence, Carlton House, with a new summer villa in Regent's Park. The new street, which was cut through some of the West End's dingiest alleys, was built between 1817 and 1823 and is seen here before the original buildings were replaced and the scale totally destroyed (see plate 306).

82. Regent Street South, looking north from Waterloo Place, c. 1885. In this view from the site of Carlton House, the original Piccadilly Circus is just visible in the distance to the right of the County Fire Office. None of these buildings has survived.

83. Regent Street, looking north from Heddon Street, c. 1860. London's most elegant shops were located between Piccadilly Circus and Oxford Circus (then known as Regent Circus North and South). On the right is the original Liberty store.

84. Looking north toward All Souls, Langham Place, c. 1860. Regent Street was terminated in the north by Nash's unusual combination of spire and circular colonnade.

82

83

84

85

86

Piccadilly Circus

85. Regent Circus South, looking east from Piccadilly, c. 1885. Nash created two elegant little circuses where Piccadilly and Oxford Street were crossed by Regent Street. This view shows the original "Piccadilly Circus" before the corner on the far left was removed in 1885 to create the shapeless space town planners have been wrestling with ever since.

86. The Quadrant, looking east toward Tichborne Street, c. 1860. The same buildings forming the north-east section of Piccadilly Circus acted as a barrier to Regent Street, forcing it to make a sharp turn in front of the County Fire Office. Much of Tichborne Street in the distance was also demolished in 1885 to make way for the construction of Shaftesbury Avenue.

87. Piccadilly Circus, looking west, c. 1895. Although the central buildings have been removed and replaced by Sir Charles Gilbert Scott's "Eros", erected in 1893, all of the buildings here are in Nash's original form except for those in the Quadrant. These had their colonnades removed in 1848 as a consequence of protests that they had become a "haunt for vice and immorality".

89

Park Lane

88. Park Lane, looking south, c. 1895.
The unusual appearance of much of Park Lane was due to the fact that many of these elevations are in fact the backs of houses in Park Street beyond. Understandably, it was one of London's finest addresses, and many famous people lived here such as the Duke of Cambridge, who occupied the building beyond the tree in the centre of this view.

89. The Green Park Arch at Hyde Park Corner, c. 1860.
When they were originally constructed in 1828, Decimus Burton's Green Park Arch and his elegant screen, which formed an inviting entrance to Hyde Park, shared a common axis, forming a link between the two parks with the traffic of Piccadilly and Knightsbridge passing between them. The Arch has since been moved to the east, aligned with Constitution Hill, and isolated on an island amid the city's busiest traffic. The rather unwieldy statue of Wellington has been replaced by the figure of Peace riding a four-horse chariot.

Westminster

90. The Houses of Parliament from the air, May 1909. Photographed from the balloon *Vivienne* at an altitude of about two thousand feet. Across the river are the seven blocks of the old St. Thomas's Hospital with Lambeth Palace and Lambeth Bridge to its right. The mass of New Scotland Yard dominates the embankment to the left of Big Ben.

91. The Houses of Parliament, looking north from Lambeth Bridge, c. 1866. Charles Barry's and August Welby Pugin's new building was the result of a competition held after the old Houses of Parliament had been destroyed by fire in 1834. Seen here shortly after its completion in 1860, and before the Embankment was constructed, it is surrounded by a jumble of wharfs and shipping.

92. Cannon Row Wharf, c. 1865. This detail is from the riverfront immediately beyond the Houses of Parliament in the previous view just north of Westminster Bridge. It is typical of the appearance of this area before the construction of the Embankment.

91

92

Further west

London continued to expand ever further west as the demand for housing increased. As it did so, villages such as Kensington and Chelsea, which had been still isolated in the 18th century, were swallowed up in its path. Although no longer separate when these photographs were taken, they still had a distinctly rural flavour.

93. Putney Bridge, looking north, c. 1880.
Similar perhaps in appearance to the original London Bridge, this old wooden pile structure was built by the king's carpenter in 1726 and survived until the mid-1880s. Beyond are Fulham Church tower, some oast-houses and a toll house spanning the bridge approach.

94. Market Court, Kensington, c. 1865.
Market Court was located just south of Kensington High Street. It was demolished in 1868.

95. The Black Lion, Church Street, Chelsea, c. 1865.
It was common for public houses like this to make the best of both worlds by combining a tea garden with their alcoholic attractions—perhaps to provide an acceptable excuse for the presence of some of their patrons.

93

95

96. Alldin's coal wharf, Chelsea, c. 1865.
Situated opposite Chelsea Old Church between
Cheyne Walk and the river. The large triangular
shovels are so shaped in order to easily penetrate the
barge's cargo of jagged lumps of coal.

97. Chelsea riverfront, c. 1865.
A scene typical of the river before the construction of
the Chelsea Embankment in 1874.

99

South of the river

98. Bishop's Walk, Lambeth, looking south, c. 1866.
Bishop's Walk ran from Lambeth Palace parallel to
the river, which is beyond the buildings on the right.
This area eventually disappeared to make way for St.
Thomas's Hospital (see plate 90).

**99. St. Mary Overy's Dock, Southwark, looking
north toward the river, 1881.** Taken by the Society
for Photographing Relics of Old London before this
area, just west of London Bridge, was demolished.

**100. The Lambeth riverfront, looking south from
Lambeth Bridge, c. 1866.** A last glimpse of the
riverside shambles as a "falling monkey" pile driver
waits to work on the new Albert Embankment. Most of
these buildings belong to the Royal Doulton Pottery
which at the time was swallowing up the many small
potteries which had traditionally existed here since
the 17th century. Two groups of kilns can be seen,
the nearer ones with their semi-circular covers open.

98

100

Rural scenes

101. The Chase, Southgate, 1906.
With two officers of the Mounted Branch on patrol.

102. Kennington Turnpike Tollgate, c. 1860.
In 1663 a law had been passed making it possible for a small toll to be charged on roads, to pay for their improvement and upkeep. By 1780 there were over twelve hundred turnpike trusts, each administering about ten miles of road. By the middle of the 19th century, however, traffic became so busy that they were abandoned and the costs paid out of general taxes. This double tollgate at Kennington lasted until 1865.

103. Highgate Tollgate, looking north, c. 1860.
The Archway, which carried Hornsey Lane over the Great North Road (now Archway Hill), was built by Nash in 1813. It was replaced by the present bridge in 1895.

104. Looking north across the fields from Belsize Lane, Hampstead, c. 1870. Running from left to right is the track leading to Hampstead now known as Fitzjohn's Avenue. In 1871 building began here and these fields gave way to the large Victorian mansions which now dominate the area.

101

102

103

104

105

105. Tooley's Farm, Hampstead, c. 1900.
Part of the Wylde estate which was bought in 1907
for construction of Hampstead Garden Suburb (see
next page).

106. The Spaniards Inn, Hampstead, c. 1900.
This 18th-century tavern is little changed today except
for the traffic which constantly attempts to squeeze
between it and the tiny 17th-century tollhouse on the left.

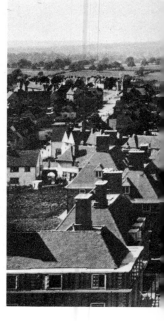

The disappearing countryside

107. Orchard Road, Plumstead, c. 1910.
Critics of every age complain bitterly of the uniformity of their architecture and crave for a return to the picturesqueness of the past. These terraces, which time has since had a chance to mellow, were once the epitome of unrelieved repetition, as this treeless and barren vista clearly demonstrates.

108. A suburban terrace under construction, c. 1900.
"LET" signs have been rather crudely added to the windows on this print to make the point that, because the demand for housing was so high, all were taken before completion.

109. Erskine Hill, looking north from the Free Church, during construction of Hampstead Garden Suburb, c. 1911. In 1898 Ebenezer Howard put forward his original idea for a "garden city" in which everyone would have equal access to light, air and open space. Based on this principle work began on the original 243-acre estate (see previous page) of Hampstead Garden Suburb in 1907. The buildings on the left are by Lutyens, and those beyond by several of the other original suburb architects: Raymond Unwin, Geoffrey Lucas, Courtenay Crickmer and Herbert Welch.

107

108

109

Social Extremes

2

"Two nations between whom there is no intercourse and no sympathy; who are as ignorant of each other's habits, thoughts and feelings, as if they were dwellers in different zones or inhabitants of different planets; who are formed by a different breeding, are fed by a different food, are ordered by different manners, and are not governed by the same laws."

From "Sybil" by Disraeli.

It is difficult to view early Victorian society as other than two isolated extremes. At one end were the rich who lived in luxury, were waited on hand and foot, made all the money and decisions and passed little other than moralistic advice on to the less fortunate. At the other end were the poor. About a third of London's population lived from hand to mouth, struggling day by day to obtain the bare essentials for survival. About a third again of these were unsuccessful in doing even this, living in a state of chronic want. Worse still, the middle ground between the two extremes of rich and very poor was not always a secure haven for the more successful working class. More often than not, it was simply a brief respite from poverty that a family in their prime might aspire to before falling back into the abyss. In all, about a quarter of the population still died in a workhouse or poor law hospital. Although reform was on the way and the rise of the middle classes was to become one of the keynotes of Victoria's reign, to most of those in authority in the middle of the 19th century the social structure was still ordained by God and not to be tampered with.

110-111 Social contrasts, c. 1859.
The fact that social comments such as these could be the subject of stereo-cards for sale to the public indicates the increasing acceptance of the need for change.

Royalty

The Queen was not so much part of the social structure as above it. Most of her subjects, of whatever class, regarded her with loyal affection, and royal occasions, few as they were after Albert's death, were seized upon by all as an excellent opportunity to have a good time.

112. Buckingham Palace, from St. James's Park, c. 1895. Originally the Duke of Buckingham's house, it was reconstructed by John Nash from 1825 to 1836 in the Palladian style and called Buckingham Palace. It is seen here as it was during Victoria's reign, before its "facelift" by Sir Aston Webb in 1913.

113. A Royal Family group, c. 1863.
Edward and Alexandra, at the back, were married in 1863. The Queen still wore black in memory of Albert, who died in 1861 and whose bust dominated the entire proceedings.

114. The Queen during her Diamond Jubilee celebrations in 1897. Seen here as her carriage drew up before the steps of St. Paul's.

112

113

114

The well-to-do

115-116. The drawing-room and garden of Broom House, Fulham, 1863. At the time, this fine 18th-century home enabled the Sullivan family who lived here to enjoy the best of both worlds, in the country yet within an easy coach journey of the city. The house was pulled down in 1912 and the gardens, on the banks of the Thames, are now part of the Hurlingham Club.

117

118

122

119 120 121

In service

Service was an essential part of the social structure and offered one of the few opportunities for women in Victorian times. By the end of the 19th century, one third of all girls between fifteen and twenty were in service, earning about 28 pounds a year. The hours were long and the work gruelling, but nevertheless the girls were well-fed and clothed and had a roof over their heads.

117-121. Putting on a crinoline skirt, c. 1860.
The crinoline arrived from Paris in the mid-fifties with its hoops of horsehair and later, steel. It is doubtful if any other garment before or since has been such a reflection of the social structure, requiring, as it did, a well-trained staff to erect and dismantle it. Note that in the last picture the maid has to lean over so far to adjust the trimming around the waist that she must be suspended by a wide band of cloth fixed to the wall. These views, taken from stereo-cards, were most probably intended to titillate rather than educate, considering the moral climate of the time.

122. "Werry sorry 'm, but yer'l 'av to leave yer Krinerline outside." c. 1860. This comic picture, copied from a *Punch* cartoon, referred to a new omnibus regulation which had been introduced as a consequence of the disruption caused by women attempting to clamber onto buses wearing these contraptions.

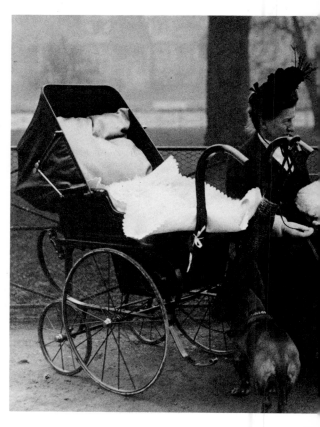

123. Nursemaid with charges in Hyde Park, c. 1900.
The little girls were so meticulously dressed for
their outing that the park bench had to be covered
to prevent them soiling their clothes.

124. Christ's Hospital kitchen, c. 1900.
Hardly domestic, but still a good indication of the
rigours of "below stairs", with a hissing copper and a
pile of coal waiting to be stoked onto the fire. Note
the naked fishtail gas jets.

**125. Maids at the First Avenue Hotel, High
Holborn, 1892.** The hot water can being carried by
the girl on the left was typical when bathrooms with
running water were still a rarity.

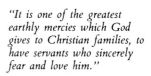

*"It is one of the greatest
earthly mercies which God
gives to Christian families, to
have servants who sincerely
fear and love him."*

*The Rev. W.B. Mackenzie
of Holloway, 1866.*

123

124

125

Making a living

126. The Consols office, The Bank of England, 1894.
Employment in the City, at whatever level, was considered one of the finest careers. The superiority of their position is certainly evident in the expressions of these young men. This room is part of Sir John Soane's original bank interior, demolished between 1924 and 1939.

127. The Wells Engineering Works, Croydon, c. 1900.

128. A workshop and forge, Islington, c. 1905.

129. A wood engraver and his apprentice, c. 1892.

130. A bootmaker in a St. James's Street basement, c. 1875.

The summit of working-class aspirations was to be a foreman or skilled artisan earning two or three pounds a week, a very adequate income by Victorian standards. Yet it was not an easy goal to achieve. The unions and guilds and the widespread acceptance of nepotism made it very difficult to get a foot in the door.

127

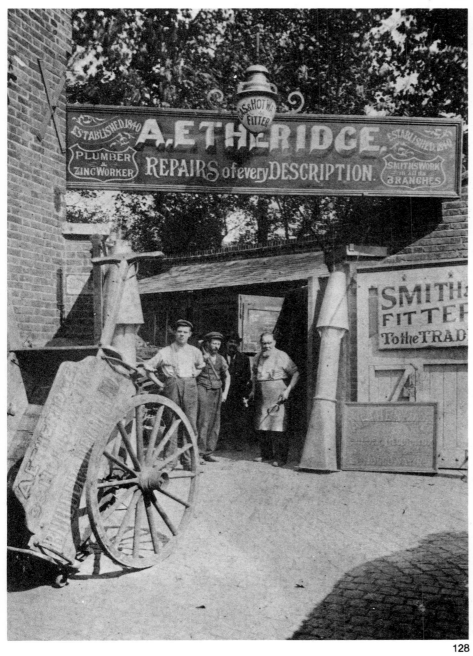

128

129

130

132

131. A second-hand furniture shop at the corner of Church Lane, Holborn, c. 1877.

132. Appleyard's Christmas poultry display, Kentish Town Road, c. 1900.

133. The Book Department of the Army and Navy Stores, Victoria Street, Westminster, c. 1900.

To keep a shop often meant that the entire family had to spend long hours behind the counter and whatever spare time they had was spent in the rooms upstairs where they usually lived. As prosperity increased, and cheaper goods became available through mass production, the demand for more shops and staff to serve in them increased dramatically. The introduction of the great department stores, such as Harrods and Selfridges, at the turn of the century, opened up enormous new possibilities for employment, especially for women.

133

134

135

136

137

134. Pea-shellers, Covent Garden Market, c. 1900.
Mary, on the left, was "Queen" of the pea-shellers, a
title she earned because of the speed at which she
had been shelling peas for fifty-six years.

**135. Sunday Bird Fair, Sclater Road, Bethnal
Green, c. 1900.** Caged birds were very popular with
the Victorians: Java sparrows, East India finches,
jays, magpies, linnets, bullfinches, goldfinches, and
parrots of all descriptions.

136. A Covent Garden porter, 1915.
How many baskets a porter could carry on his head
was always a matter of great prowess and competition.

137. Billingsgate fish porters, c. 1892.
The characteristic and very odd headgear was in fact
a padded platform which put the weight of the very
heavy boxes of fish (or anything else for that matter)
onto the porter's shoulders rather than his head,
which was simply used to keep the whole contraption
in position.

138. Covent Garden, 1909.
The arrival of the annual walnut harvest.

"Find out a prime thirsty spot, which you know by the number of public 'ouses it supports. Oysters, whelks and liquour go together inwariable; consequence where there's fewest stalls and most publics is the choicest spot for a pitch."

Quoted by Thompson and Smith in their book "Street Life in London", from which plate 139 is taken, as the words of the shellfish seller.

140

141

143

142

Those who lacked the capital for a shop could still perhaps find enough money to buy or rent a barrow or stall. If funds would not stretch even that far, the only recourse was to carry everything on a yoke, as milkmen often did, or in a basket or tray.

139. A shellfish stall, c. 1877.
Although the proprietors of such stalls were known universally as "coster-mongers" the term properly referred only to fruit-sellers.

140. Ginger cakes, King Street, Greenwich, 1884.

141. Rabbits, Greenwich, 1885.

142. Pie-maker, Greenwich Church Passage, 1885.

143. The cat's meat man, c. 1903.
It is strange that in these slum streets East Enders could still afford a penny a dozen for scraps of horse meat for their cats. Even stranger, considering that these cat's meat men would often be seen throwing scraps away for free. The wooden ER on the wall is presumably a remnant of the festivities when Edward VII was crowned in 1902.

145

146

147

148

144. A boardman advertising fabric cleaner, c. 1877.

145. A chair-caner and umbrella-mender, c. 1877.

146. A knife-grinder in the City of London, c. 1892.

147. A window-mender, King Street, Greenwich, 1885.

148. A chimney-sweep, c. 1877.

By being in the right place at the right time, rather than by establishing a regular clientele, street traders of every description offered their services in the hope of earning a shilling or so. The distinctive cries that announced their arrival, and inevitably attracted the interest of swarms of small children, were an essential ingredient in the character of old London.

149. Matches, bootlaces, pipecleaners and collarstuds, 1915. The end of the line for the self-employed was the peddling of a few items which, although of little value or profit in themselves, might bring in a few extra coppers in charity from a generous passer-by.

150. News-vendors, Charing Cross, c. 1895.

151. An apple woman, Cheapside, c. 1895.

152. A flower girl, Regent Street, c. 1895.
For many years the flower girls were one of the most picturesque sights of London, although not all were as young and pretty as this one. Every morning, very early, they would congregate around the tea stall in Covent Garden for breakfast, buy whatever flowers were left over after the florist's shops had taken their pick, and make their way to their pitches all over London.

150

149

151

153

153. A dancing bear, 1895.
These massive beasts, a common sight in residential streets in Victorian times, were traditionally owned by Italians and Spaniards. They were often cruelly treated, reduced to submission by being starved, and were frequently crammed, three or four at a time, into tiny cellars at night.

154. Street musicians, King Street, Greenwich, 1884.

155. Dancing to the organ, c. 1892.

156. Italian street musicians, c. 1877.

154

"There is one beautiful sight in the East End, and one only, and it is the children dancing in the street when the organ grinder goes his round. It is fascinating to watch them, the new-born, the next generation, swaying and stepping . . . weaving rhythms never taught in dancing school. . . But there is a Pied Piper of London who steals them all away."

From "People of the Abyss" by Jack London, 1903.

158

159

157. A home industry "blacksmith", c. 1905.

158. Making hairbrushes, c. 1905.

159. Making matchboxes, c. 1905.

Hidden from public view, in the dens and alleys of the East End, poverty created the perfect conditions for exploitation. In "sweatshops" and by means of "home industry" entire families slaved away for fourteen hours a day at such tasks as sewing jackets for fourpence each, or making matchboxes at "tuppence ha'penny" a gross. Despite the growing trades union movement in the late 19th century, it was not until the Sweated Industries Exhibition of 1906 that these conditions were finally exposed and Parliament was prompted to eliminate some of the more flagrant instances.

160. A blind beggar at a cattle market, c. 1892.

160

Poverty

In 1885, 59 percent of the adult male population earned less than 25 shillings a week, the level at which a family could just about survive and remain productive. Below this level the hand to mouth existence of poverty began. In the East End of London these statistics were irrelevant, for here poverty was universal.

161. Waiting for the pawnshop to open, c. 1900. In 1900 there were 692 pawnshops like this within a ten-mile radius of the Royal Exchange. Each handled about five thousand pledges a month, more than six a year for each member of the local population.

162. The corner of Duval Street and Crispin Street, near Spitalfields Market, c. 1912. Along with the pawnshop, the pub was the other essential facility of the East End. Victorians constantly moralised about "demon drink" and cited it as one of the major causes of poverty. But who could condemn a family, forced to crowd together in the filth and squalor of a single tiny room, for seeking relief and company in the corner pub? In any event, the many families who spent over one-sixth of their meagre income on beer would still have been poor however they had spent it, and in many cases the beer provided better nutrition than much of the food they were forced by circumstances to eat.

"A noticeable thing in poor streets is the mark left on the exterior of the houses. All along the front, about on a level with the hips, there is a broad dirty mark, showing where the men and lads are in the constant habit of standing, leaning a bit forward, as they smoke their pipes, and watch whatever may be going on in the street, while above and below the mortar is picked or kicked from between the bricks."

A quotation from one of Charles Booth's collaborators, c. 1895.

164

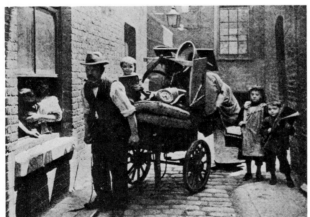

163

165

163. Providence Place, Stepney, 1909.

164. Eyre Street Hill, looking north, 1907.
Poverty was often synonymous with immigrants, of which there were many in London. While the East End was traditionally the home of the Jews, the Italians formed their own colony of "Little Italy" just to the east of Gray's Inn Road. Although many started off poor, they often rose to success as proprietors of barrel-organs, hurdy-gurdies and icecream-stalls or as fortune-tellers or ice-merchants. The establishment on the corner of Summers Street on the right illustrates such a case.

165. On the move in the East End, c. 1900.
This cart probably carries all the belongings that this family will be able to cram into the single room to which they are moving.

166. Albury Street, Deptford, 1911.
The appearance of some of the residents, and the arrival of an "Electric Palace" at the end of the road, point to a changing way of life. Notice the filth in the street, evidence of the considerable horse traffic still common at this time.

166

167. A London slum in 1889.
The dirt of the street formed a communal meeting
place for these slum dwellers. In it the children
played, the animals were kept, the washing was done
and the neighbours could gossip. That was, in fine
weather. When it rained, everything, with perhaps the
exception of the chickens, had to be crammed into
the practically windowless rooms beyond.

168. A rush on the baker's cart in the East End, c. 1910.

169. A striker's family in the East End, 1912.
London had practically no trades unions until the late 1880s when often violent demonstrations by the unemployed and strikes by such groups as the dockers and the employees of Bryant and May's match factory established new rights for workers. Despite the improvements in pay and conditions that this rebellion achieved, it temporarily strained the already inadequate resources of the poor even further.

170. A single-room home in the East End, 1912.
In this tiny room the entire family slept, cooked, ate and made their recreation. Note the home-made dartboard, the naked gas jets and the paraffin lamp on the mantel. One may speculate that perhaps the photographs gazing down from the walls were mementos of better times.

171. A single-room home in Bethnal Green, c. 1900.

"God has appointed from the very first, that there should be different grades of human society, high and low, rich and poor, and it is not for the rich to boast or the poor to complain."

The Vicar of a rural Kentish village, 1871.

169

170

Children

The children of the poor were often sorry creatures. Many of them unwanted, they placed an even further burden on the family's insufficient resources. If the mother was out working, they had to be looked after by elder children or if on their own, they were often pacified by being drugged with "Godfrey's Cordial" or some other concoction of opium and treacle from which many died. Infant mortality was very high and only about half of the children who survived birth ever lived to the age of twenty. As soon as they were old enough, they were put to earning a few pennies for the family in a local factory or pinned to their mother's knee, helping with the sewing or matchbox glueing.

172. A mother and child in a London doorway, c. 1877.

173. Two new arrivals from the East End at the Birley House open-air school, 1909.

175

176

177

178

179

Gipsies

179. A group of Gipsies, c. 1910.

180. A Gipsy family at Battersea, c. 1877.
Many Gipsies established themselves within the
bricks and mortar of the urban areas, often finding
semi-permanent plots of vacant land on which to
camp. The authors of the collection of photographs
from which this view is taken, J. Thomson and
Adolphe Smith, record that the woman sitting on the
steps, whose name was Mary Pradd, was murdered a
few weeks after the photograph was taken.

3

John Lawson
27 July 1875
361.

John Hayes
31 July 1875.
362

Lang
Aug 1875.
363

John Horner
9 Aug 1875.
365

Rob⁺ Isaacs
11 Aug 1875.
366.

M.A. Williams
14 Aug 1875
367.

Williams (Group)
14 Aug 1875.
369.

John Connor
14 Aug. 1875
370.

Sheffi

She

John Gough
3 Aug 1875

364

Eliz.ᵗʰ Williams
14 Aug 1875.

368.

...h 18 Aug 1875

71

...rough 18 Aug 1875

72.

Reform

The rapid expansion in the 19th century caught London unprepared. Poverty, crime, disease and despair had been widespread even before then, but as the population and sheer physical size of the metropolis increased these problems reached epidemic proportions. The Victorians responded with characteristic zeal and by the turn of the century had developed well organised police, fire, and sanitation services. Gleaming new stone hospitals, and red brick board schools were to be seen everywhere. In the streets the Salvation Army and members of other organisations (such as Dr. Barnardo's) were busy fighting to eliminate the desperate effects of poverty and destitution. Such reform, however, did not take place without a struggle. The associated philosophy that the key to success was through individual effort, no matter what one's origin, was a direct contradiction of the prevailing "know your place" structure of a society based upon patronage, privilege and influence. By the late 19th century the foundation stones of a new social order had been laid. A new generation of Victorians were growing up. These were men and women who were not about to be left out of a share of the fruits of the most prosperous nation in the world. While the tattered rags of the East end did not disappear, the ranks of neatly dressed, starched and ironed middle-class Londoners dominated the arrival of the new century.

181. A page from the photographer's record file, Dr. Barnardo's Home for boys, Stepney Causeway, 1875.
With the support of Lord Shaftesbury, Dr. Barnardo opened his first boys' home at Stepney Causeway in 1871. In order to keep a record of the children he helped, and also to publicize the appalling circumstances of the destitute, he opened a photographic department in 1874. Between then and the time of his death in 1905 over 55,000 photographs were taken.

182

"If you have not sunk to such despair as to be willing to barter your liberty for the sake of food, clothing and shelter in the workhouse, but are only temporarily out of employment seeking work, then you go to the casual ward 'where things are made' as disagreeable as possible . . . in order to deter you from again accepting the hospitality of the rates . . . "

From "In Darkest England" by William Booth, Founder of the Salvation Army.

183

184

182. Women picking oakum, c. 1885.
Under the Poor Law, the State accepted the
responsibility for providing food and shelter for every
destitute man, woman and child. In the casual wards
women were required to pick two pounds of oakum in
the course of their stay of two nights and one day,
while the men were required to break stones.

183. Slum sisters visiting a poor family, c. 1890.
Salvation Army "slum sisters" lived, in pairs, in the
same conditions as the poor they served. They visited
the sick, showed women how to care for themselves
and their families in general, and were concerned
with "cultivating peace, advocating temperance,
counselling in temporalities, and ceaselessly
preaching the religion of Jesus Christ".

**184. Salvation Army men's shelter, Burne Street
Metropole, Edgware Road, 1891.** These otherwise
homeless men slept in rows of egg boxes with only a
mattress stuffed with dried seaweed and an
"American leather" bedcover for comfort.

**185. Pauper children waiting for Salvation Army
farthing breakfasts, 1880.**

The destitute

187

186

188

With typical optimism, the Victorians were confident that providing health services for everyone and developing medical technology would alleviate or even eradicate the diseases that caused so much misery.

186. An operation at Charing Cross Hospital, 1901. Lister had made surgery safer with his discovery of antiseptics in 1865; a "miracle" subsequently replaced by aseptic surgery.

187. St. Thomas's Hospital, Albert Embankment, c. 1895. The second oldest hospital in London, St. Thomas's was founded in Southwark early in the 13th century and transferred to the Albert Embankment in 1871. One observer suggested that its chief ornament, "a row of hideous urns upon the parapet, seems waiting for the ashes of the patients inside" (See plate 90).

188. Goodman's Dental Establishment, looking west down Ludgate Hill from St. Paul's, 1900. There was little that Goodman wouldn't do for the Victorian mouth. Anything from one tooth to a full set was available from this very enterprising dentist.

189. Crèche, Albury Street, Deptford, 1911.

With the Act of 1870 the Victorian state expressed its desire to establish elementary schools for every child in the country. Ten years later, elementary education became compulsory for everyone. By the 70s and 80s there was hardly a child in England who did not experience at least some of the civilising influence of one of the schools set up and administered by the new local school boards. For the children of the poor, the schools not only provided much needed education but also a comfortable refuge from the misery of their home environment. By the end of the 19th century, most Londoners could read and write and do simple arithmetic, preparing them, at least minimally, for an increasingly complex world.

Education

190. School playground, c. 1865.

191. Old gallery class, c. 1890.

192. Maypole at the John Ruskin School, Beresford Street (now John Ruskin Street), S.E.5., 1908.

One of the underlying principles of the educational system at the turn of the century was uniformity. Teaching was done by rote; children were praised for precision, and individuality was by no means encouraged. In spite of this display of rigidity on the one hand, the Victorians showed admirable imagination and far-sightedness on the other in creating schools for children with special needs.

193. Numbers class, Hugh Myddleton School, 1906. Arithmetic was taught by stick-laying. In this case a flowerpot shape (note the example on the teacher's desk) represents four. The artwork around the walls (see also the previous page) demonstrates the Victorian belief that accuracy, not imagination, was what was called for.

194. Birley House open-air school, Forrest Hill, July 1908. These children and their teachers are preparing what would seem to be a wholesome enough meal. The children who attended this day school were described as "mildly chesty" and it was hoped that the fresh air would improve their condition.

195. Montpelier House open-air school, 1908.

193

194

The photographs on this page explain, as no words can, the kind of education that was deemed important for women of the period. A woman's role was clearly established and understood by all: girls were taught to be wives and mothers and how to manage a household; whether it would eventually be their own home or that of their employers made little difference.

196. Cooking class, Clapham Secondary School, 1910. The information on the blackboard tells us that the girls are preparing a meat and potatoes dinner for a family of seven.

197. Hortensia Road School, 1911.

198-199. Learning the domestic arts, Morden Terrace School, 1908. While one girl cleans the fire irons, the other polishes the table to such a commendable gloss that her reflection can be seen in it. The pictures on the walls were consistent with the fashion of the time, either framed texts or views of an uplifting nature. Notice the spotless coal-fired stove. Besides providing an oven and a cooking surface hot water could be drawn from the boiler (with the tap) on the right.

197

196

198

199

200. Engineering class, Tollington Park Central School, 1915. While the girls carried out their domestic tasks the boys were learning some very different skills. In this workshop three of them are labouring on massive foot-operated lathes not unlike treadle sewing machines.

201. Art class, Battersea Polytechnic, 1907. The importance of further education was being increasingly recognized at the time this photograph was taken. Again, it is accuracy, not imagination that is being stressed, as these young women are concentrating all of their energies on reproducing an identical likeness of a *fleur de lis*.

202

Votes for women

Although women experienced injustices at all levels of society, it was the vote that became their rallying point in the last twenty years of the 19th century. In 1900, Mrs. Garnett Fawcett formed the National Union of Woman's Suffrage Societies. In 1903, Mrs. Emmeline Pankhurst and her daughter Christabel, a law graduate, broke from Mrs. Fawcett's group and formed a militant faction called the Women's Social and Political Union. By 1905 the Union began interrupting political meetings and by 1908 all-out militancy was declared. One suffragette slashed a Velazquez *Venus* in the National Gallery, some turned to arson and others ripped the clothes off cabinet ministers. Over a thousand went to prison, many going on hunger strikes and suffering hideously from their jailers' attempts to force feed them.

202. Anti-suffrage speaker, c. 1911.

203. Sylvia Pankhurst addressing a crowd, 1912.
Thousands of women were stirred by the speeches of Mrs. Pankhurst and her daughters, Christabel and Sylvia. In this photo, however, Sylvia's audience seems to be made up almost entirely of young boys. Note that on the sign painted above the storefront the word "women" in "votes for women" has been changed to read "men".

Police

As London grew so did the opportunity for crime. In 1749 Henry Fielding formed "The Bow Street Runners". But it was not until 1829 that Sir Robert Peel's Metropolitan Police Act created the beginnings of today's organized regular police force.

204-205. Constables from Blackheath Road Police Station, Greenwich, 1885.

206. Great Scotland Yard, Westminster, c. 1880. This building at 4 Whitehall Place served as Headquarters for the Metropolitan Police from 1829-90 until they moved to new quarters on the Embankment (see plate 90) taking with them the name "Scotland Yard" with which they had become so firmly associated.

207. A Thames Police Station hulk, Victoria Embankment, c. 1866. The riverfront, with its associated commerce, was always a focus for London's criminal population. In 1797 the Marine Police were formed to protect ships from pilfering and by 1829 when the Metropolitan Police came into existence had three stations, one on land and two, conveniently situated, in old hulks on the river.

204

205

206

207

Prisons

208. Convict ship at Greenwich, 1860.
For many years the otherwise useless remains of old men-of-war were used as convenient, and isolated, repositories for society's unwanted elements. Up to five hundred convicts were often shackled in these hulks.

209. Women convicts, Pentonville Prison, c. 1860.
Pentonville was built in the 1830s as a model prison with five wings radiating from a central hall. Here, the inmates were making mosaics for St. Paul's Cathedral.

210-211. Newgate Prison, exterior and entrance hall, c. 1902. Newgate was rebuilt by George Dance the Younger, from 1770 to 1778, on the site of an earlier prison dating from the 12th century. It was demolished in 1900 to make way for the Central Criminal Court.

212. Wormwood Scrubs Prison, c. 1900.
This prison, completed in 1890, was built entirely by convicts on the site of a famous duelling ground. First, nine prisoners who were housed in a corrugated iron hut, built a temporary prison for fifty, those fifty built a prison for a hundred who in turn built the final structure.

209

210

"By the light of torches, we saw the black Hulk lying a little way from the mud of the shore, like a wicked Noah's Ark. Cribbed and barred and moored by massive rusty chains, the prison ship seemed to my young eyes to be ironed like the prisoners."

From "Great Expectations" by Charles Dickens.

211

212

Fire

Although fire had plagued the city since its founding, it took a major disaster to finally convince Parliament that a government-financed fire service was needed. In June 1861 three acres of warehouses filled with food and silks caught fire in Tooley Street near London Bridge. Besides destroying valuable commercial property, the fire took the life of James Braidwood, chief of the existing force of horse-drawn engines that were financed by private insurance companies. Braidwood's inadequate brigade, unable to find the water mains, had watched helplessly as eight buildings burned to the ground. It took five more years before committee recommendations and various other elements of the bureaucracy could be resolved, but the Metropolitan Fire Brigade was finally established in 1866. By 1869 it consisted of 50 fire-engine stations and 420 firemen including the chief officer. This force handled 1,659 fires in all, of which 170 were considered "serious".

213. Members of the London County Council Metropolitan Fire Brigade at Bread Street fire, 1899.

214. Fire at Her Majesty's Theatre, 6 December 1867.

L.S.&P.Co.

Public services

215. Dustcart, Old Montague Street, c. 1890.

216. Postman, King Street, Greenwich, 1885.

217. Cleaning a gas lamp, c. 1900.
At the beginning of the 19th century the faint flicker of oil lamps provided the only light on the streets. The advent of gas light in 1810 was a much welcomed event. Besides making London a much cheerier place, they did much to drive away the previously considerable dangers of walking alone after dark. Lamplighters became a familiar sight as they walked the streets at dusk and dawn with their long poles.

218. Police testing for river pollution, Wapping, c. 1890.
Although Parliament made it illegal to connect new drains with the river in 1870, the Thames was still described as "black and putrid" in 1880.

219. Workmen at lunch, c. 1900.
Due to the considerable punishment that the roads received from hundreds of thousands of steel-rimmed wheels and iron horseshoes, they were constantly being resurfaced. The old granite setts were replaced in most busy areas with wood block pavings to help deaden the noise.

216

217

218

219

4
Iron and Steam

Although the Industrial Revolution began in the late 18th century, it was not until Victoria's reign that its widescale application took place. Steam engines provided hitherto unimagined power, and iron and steel were used to forge the massive equipment they operated. Together they hissed and thundered to produce, at an ever rapid pace, goods for an increasingly prosperous and demanding population. Later on, the magic of electricity and the more doubtful attributes of the internal combustion engine placed this power into the hands of the individual. For the Victorians this was not simply a utilitarian development; it was a heroic and romantic odyssey into a utopian future. The potential miracles of science and technology were boundless. With them they would rid the world of want, disease and misery. No practical problem was insurmountable. Machines were built that would travel on and under land and water and even in the air. Bridges were built, tunnels were dug, towers were raised, and thousands upon thousands of ingenious devices were created in fulfilment of the new dream.

220. A motor cab overtaking a hansom, 1907.

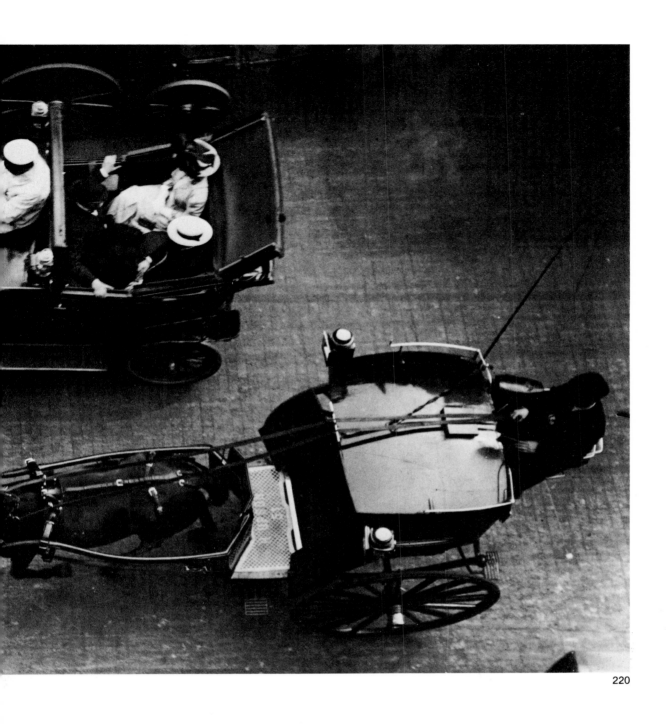

The disappearing horse

Until the middle of the 19th century the only way to travel at a speed greater than a walk was by horse.

221. Traffic on London Bridge, c. 1900.
There must be over fifty horses in this photograph pulling every kind of vehicle imaginable. In the foreground alone are farmers' carts, a mail van, several hansoms and a growler, some horse-buses and an ice-cart.

222. A London hansom cab, c. 1877.
Invented by the architect Joseph Aloysius Hansom in 1834, the hansom cab gained immediate popularity. The driver seldom left his perch from which he could communicate with his passengers by means of a trapdoor in the roof, and allow them entry and egress by means of doors in front of the seat which he controlled with a lever (see plate 76).

223. A passenger's view from a hansom, c. 1905.
This unusual photograph shows the driver's reins and the fare sheet. Generally it cost two shillings to take a hansom anywhere within four miles of Charing Cross and double that rate beyond.

224. A street accident, c. 1892.

222

223

"*You always knew when summer had arrived in London by the smell of lime flowers, horse dung and melting tar.*"

From an interview with Sir Osbert Lancaster.

224

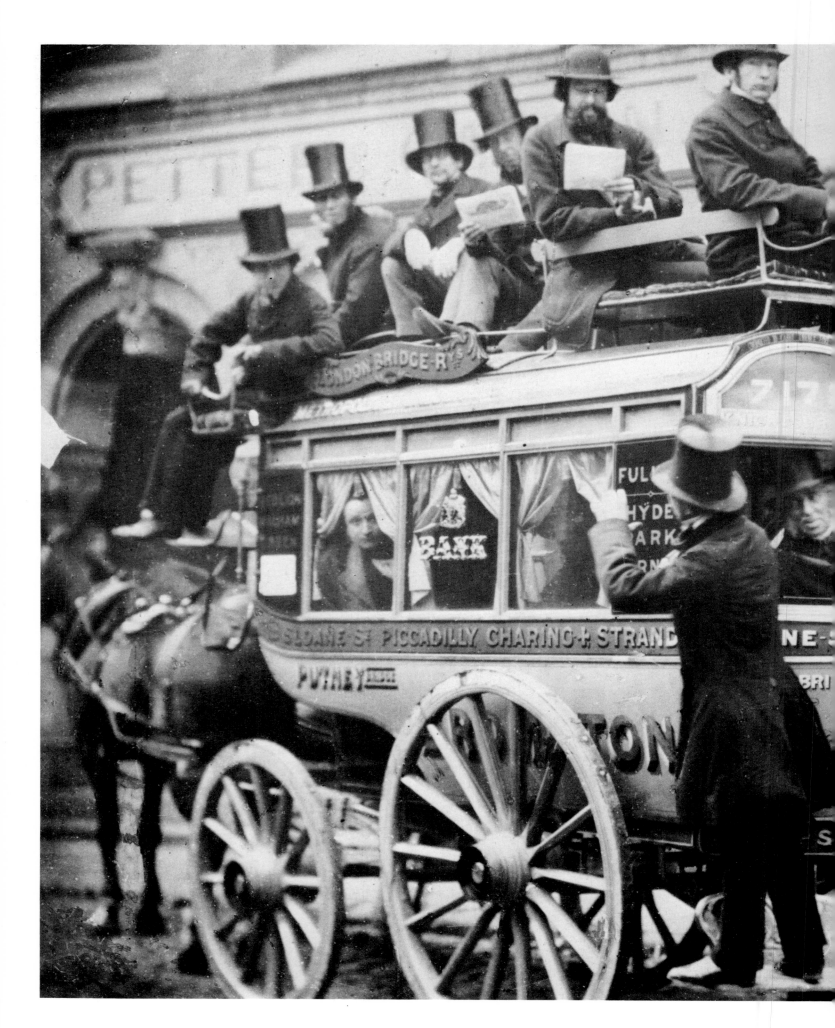

George Shillibeer introduced the first horse-bus to Londoners in 1829. By the 1840s they were a common sight and in addition to their interior accommodations were beginning to develop some means for assisting passengers who could not jam themselves inside to clamber on top. The famous "knifeboard" bus followed, where two rows of passengers could sit back to back on the roof. In the 1880s some stairs and forward-facing "garden-seats" were added (see plate 221), providing the penultimate step in the evolution of today's double-deckers.

225. A saloon bus, c. 1858.
With far more passengers outside than in, these, and many other types of vividly painted and gilt-lettered horse-buses rumbled over the streets of London day and night. In the early days in particular they were owned and operated by several different private companies, which added to their variety and colour.

226. An omnibus and its driver, c. 1877.
The rather formidable gentleman on the left was a famous employee of the Thomas Tilling Company known as "Cast Iron Billy".

227. A London horse-bus stable, c. 1885.

228. "B" type buses in a London garage, 1911.

229. Traffic at the Elephant and Castle, 1912.

The problems of urban transportation provided an ideal focus for the ingenuity of turn-of-the-century engineers. Before long the protesting (and often terrified) public were being hauled around by a bewildering array of whirring, wheezing, clattering and more explosive devices. In this view alone there are a National paraffin-fired steam bus, an L.C.C. electric tram, and a General "B" type petrol-bus. Dwarfed by them all is one of the remaining horse-buses. The first electric tram had been introduced in 1901 and the first fleet of two hundred motor-buses in 1905. Only a few years later, in 1916, the last horse-bus would be driven from the streets of London.

"It is true that the sulphurous atmosphere is far from pleasant, but there is no reason to suppose that it is seriously injurious to the health. In fact, there are those who have discovered medicinal virtues in it, and although the Inner Circle has not yet become a resort of valetudinarians, the experience of the companies' servants tends to show that there is nothing specially deleterious in the conditions of their labour."

From "Living London", regarding the Metropolitan Railway.

230

231

232

The railway from Manchester to Liverpool was opened in 1830, and the one from London to Birmingham in 1838. By the 1840s bridges, tunnels, viaducts, cuttings and embankments were advancing everywhere. By 1850 over six thousand miles of track were in operation.

230. Head guard, South Eastern Railway, Lewisham, 1885.

231. Construction of St. Pancras Station, c. 1867.

232. Construction of the Metropolitan Railway Station at Kings Cross, looking north, 1862.

233. Kingsbury and Neasden Station, c. 1895.
On 10 January 1863, the world's first underground railway, the Metropolitan, was opened from Paddington to Farringdon Street. Passengers were confined in a tunnel, together with all the smoke, steam, and uproar of the engine which pulled the carriages. Understandably, it was not until the introduction of electricity that the deep tubes really became practicable. As the Metropolitan was extended northwards it removed the last obstacle to the rapid expansion of the city.

234. Guests bound for the King's garden party at Windsor, Paddington Station, 1912.

235. A family leaving for a seaside holiday, Waterloo Station, 1913.

Ships

Until 1870 sailing-ships were still the fastest and most economical vessels to move the resources of the greatest empire on earth. But, with the opening of the Suez Canal in 1870 which the clippers were unable to navigate, the ingenuity of the Victorians was turned to making the slower steamships more efficient.

236. Building of the liner *Tancore*, 1865.

237. Richard Tangye posing below one of the paddle wheels of the *Great Eastern*, 1858. In spite of her builders' high expectations, this massive ship never made a profit—some say the rumor of a ghost on board frightened passengers away. Retired from passenger service in 1865, the *Great Eastern* was converted for use as a cable-layer.

238. The heavy turnery, Penn and Son, Greenwich, c. 1855.

239. Woolwich Ferry, 1902.
In order to accommodate the considerable variation in the tides of the Thames, the platform of this ferry could be raised and lowered to the level of the quayside.

240. The Rev. G. W. Garrett's submarine, 1879.

237

239

240

238

Aircraft

Of all of the technological advances of the turn of the century, nothing captured the imagination of the public more than the conquest of the air. Balloons had existed since the 18th century but it was not until the 20th century that their popularity mushroomed into a craze. When heavier-than-air craft became a reality the early enthusiasts could be found building their own machines, most of which actually flew, in garages, workshops and even attics, all over the country.

241. A ballooning scene at Hurlingham, c. 1908.
Balloon meets such as this and the one held at Ranelagh were very fashionable affairs, and, until World War I, were all the rage among the rich. The more adventurous women of the upper classes found much to recommend "balloonacy", as some of the less enthusiastic dubbed it. These women considered the sport far more feminine than motoring and were quite taken by its elegance and excitement.

242. Louis Noel in a Maurice Farman biplane rounding pylon no. 1 at Hendon, 1914.

243. A Morane Saulnier about to take off at Hendon, 1913.

Engineering

244.-245. Construction of the Holborn Viaduct, 1869.
The steepness of Holborn as it crossed the Oldbourne
Valley had been an issue for centuries, as it brought
any heavily laden cart or bus to a virtual standstill. In
1863 construction had begun on a quarter-mile-long
viaduct to alleviate the problem. It was opened by the
Queen in 1869 on the same day she opened the new
Blackfriars Bridge. Despite the steam engine in the
foreground which was revolutionising industry and
construction, it was still the British "navvies" (short
for navigators—or canal builders) who were providing
the muscle for turning the Victorian dream into a
reality. They were so well thought of in Europe that
they were paid double rates when building the railway
from Berlin to Hamburg.

246

THAMES IRON WORKS &
SHIP BUILDING Co BLACKWALL

247

249

246. The Earl's Court wheel under construction, 1894.

247. The Blackwall Tunnel under construction, c. 1890.

248. Tower Bridge under construction, c. 1890.
In best Victorian tradition the advanced hydraulic
machinery that operated this double drawbridge was
housed in a Gothic exterior. In his praise for the
bridge and the English who built it, one Frenchman
extolled: "No other people know how to unite with the
same harmonious force the cult of the past, the
religion of tradition, to an unchecked love of progress
and a lively and insatiable passion for the future."

**249. The Victoria Embankment under
construction, c. 1870.** Sir Joseph Bazalgette,
engineer to the Metropolitan Board of Works, oversaw
the building of the Victoria Embankment as well as
the Albert Embankment on the other side of the river
(see plates 91, 100, 207). Within it were one of the
three east-to-west sewers designed to help clean up
the river, water and gas mains, telephone lines and
the Circle Line underground tunnel. Here, the view of
St. Paul's is unobstructed except for two gasholders
which were demolished three years later.

250

250. The Crystal Palace, Sydenham, c. 1900.

251. The rebuilding of the Crystal Palace, c. 1853.

252. Interior of the Crystal Palace, c. 1860.

In many ways Paxton's design for the "Crystal Palace" (as *Punch* dubbed it) expressed the very essence of the age. Its delicate form rose to the sky like some vast cathedral dedicated to Victorian ingenuity and enterprise. Constructed to house the Great Exhibition of the Works of Industry of All Nations, it was opened in Hyde Park on 1 May 1851, and was immediately accepted as a triumph by everyone who saw it. Before the exhibition closed in October over six million people visited it from all over the world. Fears that such an influx of foreigners would mean the assassination of the Royal Family and a plague of venereal disease were happily unfounded. In 1852 it was dismantled, moved to Sydenham, re-erected and extended and was a great attraction for many years (see plates 295-296). It tragically burnt to the ground in 1936.

251

252

253

254

In 1878, Alexander Graham Bell revolutionised the entire concept of communication with his invention of "the speaking telephone". In 1879 the first exchange was opened in the City of London in Coleman Street; it had seven or eight subscribers. In less than two years this figure had risen to nine hundred. By 1910 there were over half a million telephones in Britain, mostly being used by progressive businesses.

253. Repairing overhead wires, National Telephone Company, c. 1900. Originally individual lines came in overhead to the exchanges. The standard on the Lime Street roof bore over twelve thousand wires. The National Telephone Company absorbed several smaller companies and maintained a monopoly until the Post Office took over the entire telephone system in 1911.

254. Purley Exchange, c. 1908.

255. Avenue Exchange Switchroom, c. 1910. The opening of telephone facilities did more than revolutionise communication. In social terms no other development did more to create jobs for women outside the home.

5

In the 19th century pleasure and recreation, for anyone other than the rich, was considered as somewhat of an evil, mainly because it tended to come between a man and his work. But as the century progressed and the early enterprise of the Victorians began to bear fruit, a much more relaxed attitude emerged. By the time Edward came to the throne the increasingly emancipated middle classes, including women, had earned and were demanding the freedom to take time off to enjoy the flamboyant and glittering new society of which they now felt very much a part.

256. Hyde Park, c. 1901.
For Londoners with any pretence for fashion, Hyde Park was an essential *rendez-vous*. The elegant screen at the entrance to the park was designed by Decimus Burton and erected in 1825 (see plate 89).

257. Promenading at Southend, c. 1908.
By the turn of the century more and more employers were giving their staff a day's or even a week's holiday. Southend, a three-shilling day-trip from London, was a great favourite, particularly for the less well-to-do.

At Leisure

256

257

258

259

260

Up until the recent past, life revolved very much around the home and family, whose members had to entertain themselves and each other. This was a time when the art of piano-playing, singing or reading aloud were an everyday necessity, and when the written word or an evening out at a lecture or a visit to the theatre was a much treasured contact with new ideas and the outside world.

258. An elegant *soirée*, c. 1860.

259. Family group viewing stereo-cards, c. 1865.

260. Family group around the piano, c. 1902.

261. Family group around the fire, c. 1912.
This wonderful scene sums up family life at the turn of the century; gathered around a blazing coal fire, in front of which sits trusty Fido, Father reads the paper, Mother does her needlework, while the third member of the family gazes blankly into space. Notice the antimacassars over the chairbacks, so named as they protected the furniture from the oil of macassar which was universally used to plaster hair down to a regular Edwardian neatness. Interesting also is the fabric fire-screen bracketed out from the mantelpiece.

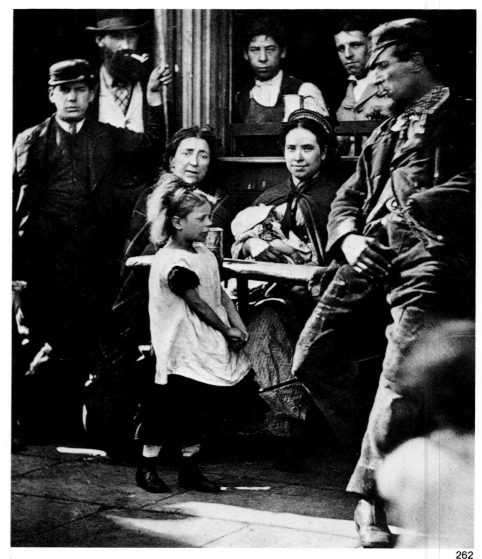

262

The pub

If there is one institution, known the world over, which is peculiar to British social life, it is the Public House. Particularly for the poor it was often more of a home than their own. At almost every street corner pubs provided a rich and vital alternative to their otherwise depressing environment. Although much criticised by the early Victorians, London pubs had become more acceptable by the 1890s and "respectable" women even began to appear in them (if accompanied by a man).

262. A pub in Whitechapel, c. 1877.
Notice the pewter tankards and clay pipes in this East End scene. The man on the right was known as "Hookey Alf", a reminder that in the 19th century a minor injury could easily result in amputation or worse.

263. The Sir Walter Raleigh, New Street, E.C.2, 1910.

264. Recruiting sergeants at Westminster, c. 1877.
One of the dangers in visiting a public house was recruitment. On many occasions the bravado and patriotism of a few pints of beer resulted not only in a hangover but a career in the Army.

263

Eating out

The turn of the century is looked upon by gourmets as a golden age. London abounded with French and Italian restaurants that spared no expense either in décor or elaborate menus. On a more modest level there were of course jellied eels, meat pies and an increasing number of establishments which catered to the army of thousands of clerks and office workers.

265. The dining-room of the Cheshire Cheese, Wine Office Court, Fleet Street, 1903. Built soon after the Great Fire, the Cheshire Cheese has many claims to fame, one being the regular patronage of Dr. Johnson and the other its great pudding, usually weighing from fifty to eighty pounds "entombed therein, beef-steak, kidneys, oysters, larks, mushrooms, and wondrous spices and gravies".

266. The "Royal Cafe", Brixton Station, c. 1910.

267. Restaurants, Aldgate, c. 1900.
The price of ordinary food was so stable that half the menu could be permanently painted on the building's exterior. Some typical examples were: Sausage, potatoes, onions and bread 4d, meat pies 2d, ham sandwiches 2d, plum pie 1d, and a cup of tea 1d.

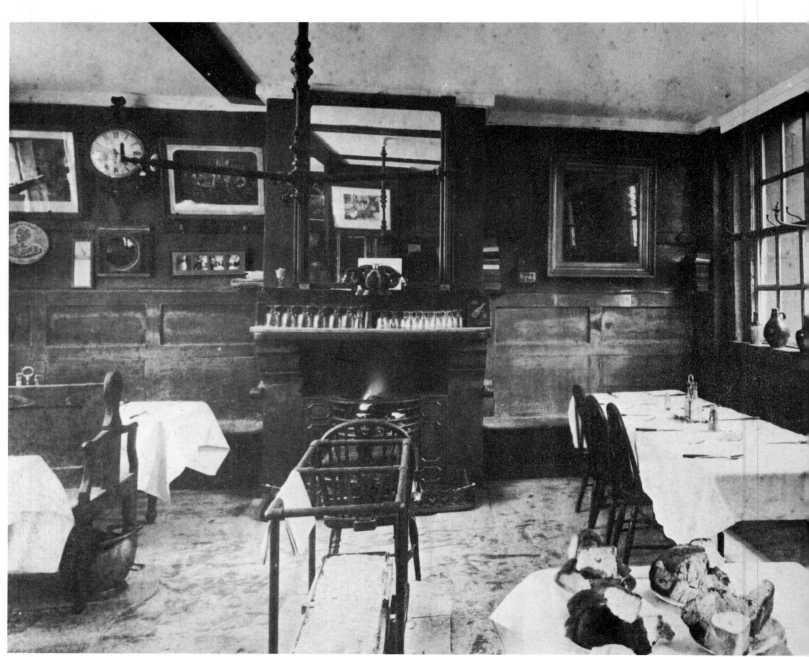

Theatre

A visit to the theatre was a very popular form of family amusement. They were gas-lit, and the accommodations varied from red plush for the wealthy to plain wooden backless benches in the "gods" for those with more enthusiasm than money. Although equally popular, music-halls were not considered fit for women due to the usually bawdy nature of the songs.

268. The old Empire, Leicester Square, 1895.
Opened in 1887 the Empire was the most notorious music-hall in London. It was, amongst other things, famous for having been the scene of a riot when, in 1894, barriers were erected between the bar and the auditorium in an attempt to end the historic custom of drinking while watching the show. It was destroyed in 1927 to make way for a cinema.

269. The Egyptian Hall, 170 Piccadilly, 1895.
The first building of this style in London, the Egyptian Hall was originally opened as a museum in 1812 and was used to display Napoleon's coach captured at Waterloo. Over the years it became a home for "unusual" entertainment and was eventually one of the first places to be used to display moving pictures. It was demolished in 1905.

270

270. A scene from *The Whip,* Drury Lane Theatre, c. 1909.
One of the most popular forms for the theatre was melodrama in which disaster was just avoided and all ended happily—although things don't seem to be going too well in this scene.

271. Mrs. Patrick Campbell, c. 1895.

272. Mrs. Patrick Campbell and Forbes Robertson in *Romeo and Juliet* at the Lyceum, 1895.

273. A "Scorcher", c. 1910.
Many figures in theatre achieved enormous popularity although it took a long time for the term "actress" to have anything other than rather disrespectful overtones. This was in part due to the rather fleeting affections of the famous "Gaiety Girls" and other "Scorchers" to whom many of the young nobility lost their hearts (and sometimes fortunes).

271

273

272

Sport

In early times sport mainly consisted of disorganised mobs propelling miscellaneous spherical objects over the landscape with variously shaped cudgels or with their feet. Another alternative involved substituting some kind of living creature for the ball. It was the Victorians who classified and formalised these activities into such games as cricket, golf, croquet, hockey, tennis and football. Thankfully they attempted to repress the crueller sports like brawling, bull-baiting, cock-fighting, rat-catching and badger-drawing. At first the involvement of women in sport was limited to cheering from the sidelines. Later on games like croquet, tennis and cycling provided a socially accepted activity for both newly thrown together sexes.

274. Two wrestlers, c. 1895.

275. Girl with hockeystick, c. 1910.

276. Bookmaker at Epsom, c. 1912.

274

275

Parks

277-278. Rotten Row, Hyde Park, 1904 and 1915.
This was the parading ground of the fashionable and
well-to-do, particularly after church on Sunday
morning when thousands of carriages proceeded,
with the object of being admired, at a snail's pace
along "The Row". The origin of the name is unknown
although it has been suggested it could have derived
from "Route du Roi".

279. Regent's Park Zoo, 1900.
The ever popular elephant is clearly used to receiving gratuities from his passengers, judging from the attitude of his trunk.

280. Skating in St. James's Park, c. 1900.
Skating on the Serpentine or in the other parks was both popular and dangerous. In 1867 forty-one skaters were drowned in Regent's Park when the ice gave way under the weight of over five hundred people. Although this was the worst ice disaster recorded, such accidents were not uncommon.

281. A group of naturalists, c. 1900.

279

280

281

282. "Mush fakers" and ginger-beer-makers, c. 1872.
The "mush faker" repaired umbrellas and was often
to be seen in the parks with a cheap second-hand
"brolly" on sale if the weather turned bad. The cart is
laden with ginger beer and "bullseyes".

283. Dancing on Hampstead Heath, 1898.
These girls had probably all been brought here on an
excursion paid for by their employer. Particularly on
Bank Holidays Hampstead Heath was the scene of
much frivolity and mischief. In the background is Jack
Straw's Castle.

284. Vale of Health pond, Hampstead Heath, 1898.

283

284

The seaside

285-288. Seaside scenes, 1900-10.
It was fairly easy for Londoners to get to the seaside by means of a steamer or *Margate Hoy* on the Thames, and even more convenient when the railway arrived. By the turn of the century the middle classes were even getting a week or two's holiday, often spent at the seaside. Although nude bathing was still common many bathers coyly insisted on using bathing-machines (the striped-wheeled vehicles on the left) which were drawn into the sea to allow the bather to slip into the water unobserved.

285

286

287

288

Special occasions

In an age without radio, television, or glossily
illustrated magazines, any opportunity to see the
famous figures of the time was eagerly seized upon
by all and sundry. Londoners would happily turn out
by the thousands, armed with picnic lunches and
paper flags, to spend an entire day propped up
against a fountain or lamp post waiting for a few
seconds' glimpse of the Queen or visiting dignitary.

**289. Piccadilly being decorated for Queen
Victoria's Diamond Jubilee, 1897.** No expense was
spared in suitably embellishing the route of the Royal
procession. This scene is also a reminder that these
were days when men were men and ladders were ladders.

**290. Looking east along Piccadilly from the top of
a bus, c. 1900.**

**291. The Canadian Arch in Whitehall, Coronation
Day, 1902.**

289

291

290

"Horray! Horray! for
Jubilation Day! 'Tis only
once in fifty years, so people
say, We all got tight, and
had a jolly spree, A' going
with the missus to the
Jubilee!"

*An old street song, taken
from "Drawn from
Memory" by Ernest H.
Shepard*

292-293. Franco-British Exhibition at the White City, 1908. This enormous fantasy-land, complete with artificial lakes and bridges, comprised the biggest exhibition ground that London had ever seen. The exotic architecture in these photographs makes it clear how the White City got its name. After World War I, during which the buildings were used for military purposes, the whole area with the exception of the sports arena remained derelict until the land was developed as a housing estate in 1936.

294. Earls Court Exhibition, c. 1895.
This view is taken from the main thoroughfare of the Italian village looking toward the massive Graydon Wheel (see plate 246).

295-296. Fireworks at the Crystal Palace, Sydenham, celebrating the Queen's Eightieth Birthday, 1899. After its re-erection at Sydenham in 1852-3 (see plates 250-252) the Crystal Palace and its considerable grounds were the frequent scene of celebrations and exhibitions of every kind. In addition to the necklace lighting which covered the building and surrounded the park, these fireworks must have been a grand spectacle reflected in the water.

295

Postscript

The first generation of Victorians, stern and harshly disciplined, had striven to thrust their country into the light of a new technological and social renaissance. The second generation had grown up in an environment of unmatched prosperity and glittering scientific miracles. Along with this came a swift, inevitable social reordering. The Edwardians lived in a London where already the rich and the poor were no longer the totality of the social spectrum, and where women had begun to take their place alongside men in the offices and stores. In 1914 men from all stations of life who would scarcely have acknowledged the existence of each other in happier times, suddenly found themselves thrown together in the mud and terror of World War I and became brothers. The jobs they had left in the factories, offices and farms were taken over by women who were ready and eager to end their historical isolation. Many lamented these changes but there could be no turning back. The Great War marked the end not only of an era but of a way of life that had existed for centuries.

297. Zeppelin caught in searchlight beams, c. 1915.

298. The wreckage of a Zeppelin brought down by the Royal Flying Corps "somewhere near London", c. 1915. At night these immense, sinister shapes menaced the city from above. Yet by the light of day the delicate structure of this burned-out airship rises as elegantly from these fields as did the Crystal Palace at Sydenham.

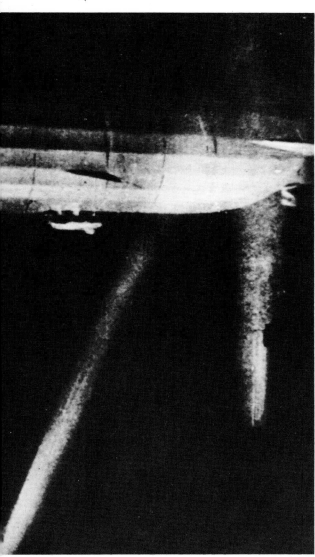

299

300

The Great War

299. Restaurant at 77 Aldgate High Street damaged in a Zeppelin attack, 1915. It was a rude awakening for Londoners that the natural isolation traditionally provided by the Channel and the North Sea was no longer a protection. The same scientific marvels which had helped bring about their prosperity were now beginning to show a more menacing side.

300. Ambulances outside Buckingham Palace, 1915.

301. White City recruiting office, 1915.
Patriotic fervour to enlist was very strong in the early days of the war when everyone expected it all to be over by Christmas. But as the months—then years—rolled by and the terrible numbers of mutilations and casualties grew, conscription had to be introduced.

302. Alexandra Palace P.O.W. compound, c. 1915.
Besides the destruction, the war changed the face of London in other, more subtle ways. In this incongruous and very British scene German prisoners of war are sunning themselves on the grassy slopes before Alexandra Palace while being observed from trellised guard-towers that would have made a charming addition to any suburban back garden.

302

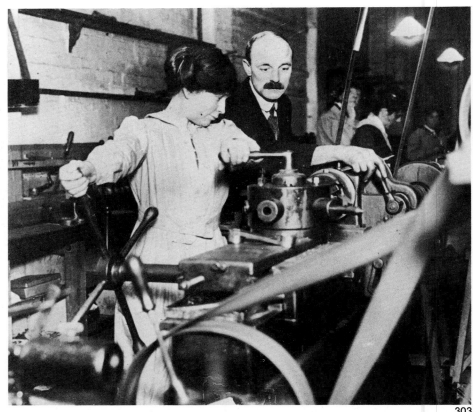

Women at war

As the men went off to the front, the women quietly and confidently took over their jobs. They stoked boilers, shovelled coal, swept chimneys, drove lorries, and not only worked in the factories but helped build them. Like it or not, and many did not, women at last had the opportunity to show Britain what they were made of. To prove the point they won the right to vote in the December election following the Armistice.

303. Shoreditch munitions class of the L.C.C. Technical Institute, c. 1915. Classes in factory work were rapidly organised at the onset of war. One wonders how many young men would have worn as confident an expression as this woman when confronted by the complexities of a capstan lathe for the first time.

304. Women brewers at Watney, Combe, Reid and Co., c. 1915.

305. Women police patrols at Euston Station, c. 1915.

306. Piccadilly Circus, looking west, c. 1913.
Only a couple of horses now gingerly thread their way
between the motor-cars and buses that crowd around
"Eros". To the left and right the original circus and
County Fire Office remain while in the centre, the first
monumental block of Norman Shaw's Quadrant
dominates the elegant and human scale of Nash's
original. A metamorphosis is taking place which will
totally change the character of the city. The throngs
of people on the pavements and in the shops along
Regent Street consist no longer of just the privileged
few. They are enjoying the fulfilment of a dream that
a century before had still seemed an impossibility.

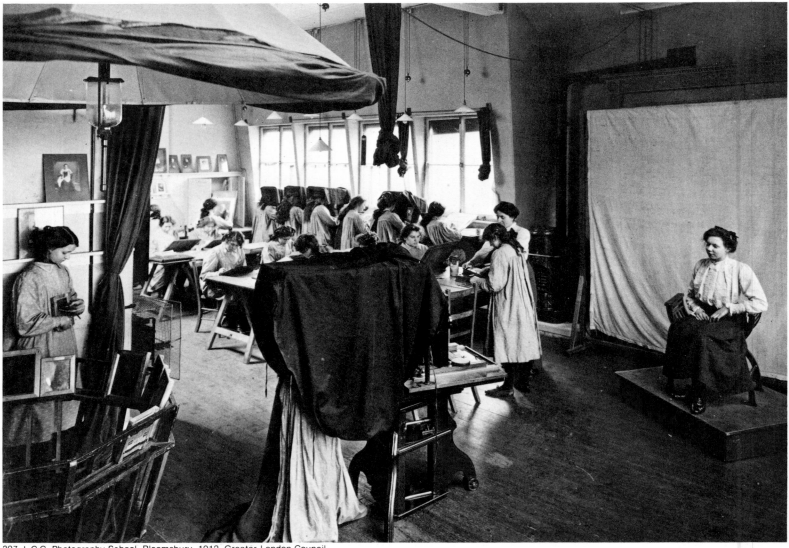

307. L.C.C. Photography School, Bloomsbury, 1912, Greater London Council.

Sources

1 **Museum of London**
  Ph. Gunn V. Stuart

2 **Victoria and Albert Mus.**
  Photographer unknown

3 **National Maritime Mus.**
  Photographer unknown

4 **Greenwich Public Library**
  Ph. Rev. Charles Spurgeon

5 **Howarth-Loomes**
  Photographer unknown

6 **Howarth-Loomes**
  Ph. Robert Howlett

7 **London Transport**
  Photographer unknown

8 **Greater London Council**
  Artist unknown

9 **British Museum**
  Modern photograph

10 **British Museum**
  Modern photograph

11 **Museum of London**
  Modern photograph

12 **Museum of London**
  Drawing by Alan Sorrell

13 **British Museum**
  Engraving by Thos. Barlow

14 **Museum of London**
  Engraving by Nicholls

15 **Museum of London**
  Engraving by Hollar

16 **British Museum**
  Engraving by Visscher

17 **Museum of London**
  Artist unknown

18 **R.I.B.A. Library**
  Etching of Sir Wren's Plan

19 **R.I.B.A. Library**
  Modern drawing

20 **R.I.B.A. Library**
  Modern drawing

21 **R.I.B.A. Library**
  Modern drawing

22 **Kodak Museum**
  From original by Kircher

23 **Science Mus., London**
  Modern photograph

24 **Kodak Museum**
  Ph. Niepce

25 **Howarth-Loomes**
  Photographer unknown

26 **Kodak Museum**
  Modern photograph

27 **Science Mus., London**
  Artist unknown

28 **Kodak Museum**
  Modern photograph

29 **Kodak Museum**
  Modern print

30 **Science Mus., London**
  Ph. Fox Talbot

31 **Science Mus., London**
  Ph. Fox Talbot

32 **Kodak Museum**
  Ph. Hill and Adamson

33 **Author's Collection**
  Photographer unknown

34 **Kodak Museum**
  Artist unknown

35 **Howarth-Loomes**
  Ph. James Robertson

36 **Howarth-Loomes**
  Ph. Mayall

37 **Howarth-Loomes**
  Modern photograph

38 **Howarth-Loomes**
  Underwood & Underwood

39 **Author's Collection**
  Modern photograph

40 **Kodak Museum**
  Modern photograph

41 **Kodak Museum**
  Modern Photograph

42 **Kodak Museum**
  Photographer unknown

43 **Kodak Museum**
  Photographer unknown

44 **Hashwood Heath Coll.**
  Photographer unknown

45 **National Martime Mus.**
  Photographer unknown

46 **Private Collection**
  Ph. J. Thomson

47 **Radio Times Hulton**
  Photographer unknown

48 **Nat'l. Monuments Record**
  Photographer unknown

49 **National Maritime Mus.**
  Photographer unknown

50 **Howarth-Loomes**
  Ph. G.W. Wilson

51 **Radio Times Hulton**
  Photographer unknown

52 **National Maritime Mus.**
  Photographer unknown

53 **Radio Times Hulton**
  Photographer unknown

54 **Tower Hamlets Pub. Lib.**
  Photographer unknown

55 **Kodak Museum**
  Ph. Griffith Brewer

56 **Guildhall Library**
  Photographer unknown

57 **Guildhall Library**
  Photographer unknown

58 **Guildhall Library**
  Photographer unknown

59 **Radio Times Hulton**
  Photographer unknown

60 **Victoria and Albert Mus.**
  Photographer unknown

61 **Victoria and Albert Mus.**
  Photographer unknown

62 **Guildhall Library**
  Photographer unknown

63 **Victoria and Albert Mus.**
  Photographer unknown

64 **Victoria and Albert Mus.**
  Photographer unknown

65 **Guildhall Library**
  Photographer unknown

66 **Guildhall Library**
  Photographer unknown

67 **Victoria and Albert Mus.**
  Photographer unknown

68 **Victoria and Albert Mus.**
  Photographer unknown

69 **Victoria and Albert Mus.**
  Photographer unknown

70 **Victoria and Albert Mus.**
  Photographer unknown

71 **Victoria and Albert Mus.**
  Photographer unknown

72 **Radio Times Hulton**
  Photographer unknown

73 **Guildhall Library**
  Ph. J. Benjamin Stone

74 **Radio Times Hulton**
  Photographer unknown

75 **Guildhall Library**
  Photographer unknown

76 **Radio Times Hulton**
  Photographer unknown

308. Entrance to London Dock, c. 1900, National Maritime Museum.

Acknowledgements

In the three years that it has taken to complete this book I have had not only the incomparable pleasure of searching through tens of thousands of photographs but also of meeting the many people who made them available to me. I would like to acknowledge the help of a few of them, not necessarily in order of importance but in the sequence with which I made their acquaintance.

Firstly, Bernard Howarth-Loomes whose generosity and considerable knowledge, particularly on the subject of early stereo-photography was invaluable. This help was doubly appreciated in the light of the fact that on several occasions it was given after I had inadvertently disturbed him trying to catch up on some sleep. It was often his habit to get up at the crack of dawn to track down some elusive pieces of early photographic equipment at Bermondsey or one of the other more remote markets in London.

Secondly, Brian Coe of the Kodak Museum, who again made not only his remarkable collection available to me, but also his inexhaustible knowledge on the subject. It should be further noted that had it not been for his efforts, many of the photographs in this book would not have survived for us to see. This help was again particularly appreciated as at the time he was very busy attempting to re-invent salt paper printing for the Fox Talbot exhibition.

In the many private collections and museums I was particularly grateful for the assistance of Elizabeth Clifford, David Francis and Patrick Beaver, Miss R. Watson and C.W. Anderson of the G.L.C. Photographic Library; David Wright of the Victoria & Albert Museum; Colin Sorensen and Oliver Green of the Museum of London; John Ward of the Science Museum; R.E. Squires and Alan Williams of the Imperial War Museum; G.N. Georgano and John Ware of the National Motor Museum at Beaulieu; John Fisher and Ralph Hyde of the Guildhall Library; Julian Watson of Greenwich Public Library; Stephen Crode and Ian Leith of the National Monuments Record; Mrs. Hannam of the Salvation Army; and Mrs. Grafton Green of the Hampstead Garden Suburb Trust.

On the publishing and editorial side many thanks are due to T.G. Rosenthal and Peter Ireland of Secker & Warburg; Susan Ann Protter and Abner Stein, my agents in New York and London respectively; Bernard Howarth-Loomes and Brian Coe again, who checked through the section on the history of photography; and John Clark and Rosemary Weinstein of the Museum of London, who made many valuable contributions to my introductory history of London; Marjorie Cohen who helped with the research and editing; and, in my New York design studio, Harriet Hoffman, who edited, proofed, corrected and cropped, and together with Laura Hart, assisted with the mechanicals.

I re-photographed most of the original material for this book on Kodak Panatomic X using a Nikon F with 55 mm Micro-Nikkor as in most instances negatives had never been made before or were unsatisfactory. The processing and printing was undertaken by Duncan Wherrett of the N.J. Paulo Laboratory in Covent Garden.

Last but not least, I am very grateful to my wife, Helga, who apart from doing most of the typing did much of the research and indexing and also found time to give birth to our young son Ben along the way. Thank you all very much.

309 Haley's Comet over St. Paul's, 1858, David Francis.